H. S. Brown

A Compendium of the Bible of the Religion of Science

H. S. Brown

A Compendium of the Bible of the Religion of Science

ISBN/EAN: 9783337171773

Printed in Europe, USA, Canada, Australia, Japan

Cover: Foto ©Lupo / pixelio.de

More available books at **www.hansebooks.com**

A COMPENDIUM

—— OF ——

THE BIBLE

—— OF THE ——

RELIGION OF SCIENCE,

—— BY ——

H. S. BROWN, M. D.,

Author of "A Permanent Republic Cannot be Established on Despotic Family Laws." "Spiritualism is the Basis of a Scientific Religion and Government," and other Works.

The Law God is the true Natural God, that agrees with the natural man, and with all the material, spiritual, mental, moral and social sciences.

The Gods of revelations or words, are made by man, and are the enemies of the natural man and the natural God; and of all the material, spiritual, mental, moral and social sciences.

PUBLISHED BY THE AUTHOR,
527 Milwaukee Street, Milwaukee, Wis.,
August, 1885.

This volume is most respectfully dedicated to those persons who will cordially unite and work together to establish a just government and the true religion by the scientific methods of Reason, Experience, Experiments and Observations. For these have proved to be the way to knowledge and wisdom, that make peace and good will among the people of the earth.

PREFACE.

This Compendium is calculated to give but little more than a summary of the texts that constitute the foundation principles of the science of association, religion and government. Wherever you have a religion that the professors claim was made by God, there must be a government made by the same God to match it; to make harmony. The only trouble among the people where they have this union of church and state is: Who shall be their rulers and priests. This part the people decide, if their gods have done all the rest. If you have a government made by man, as this United States government was, you must have a religion made by man, on humanitarian principles, to be in harmony with it. To assist people in making this religion I put forth this humble volume, hoping it will draw attention to this most important subject.

INTRODUCTION.

The question may be properly asked : Why do you propose to establish a new religion? Because there is a large class of learned, thoughtful people who have outgrown all the old religions, believe them false in pretended facts, unjust and immoral in principle, and wholly unfit to guide and give comfort to good, intelligent, independent thinking people.

It is to give comfort and joy to this large class of people, which is at present growing rapidly in all enlightened countries. This religion is especially calculated to reach and give the same consolations that the old religions give to the ignorant and superstitious. Its principles have arisen among the most enlightened people of this enlightened age, and have come to stay ; its intelligent advocates have made many important discoveries, that agree with the demonstrated knowledge of the material sciences, and are bound together in a harmonious whole, that will draw all the intelligent people into the bands of wisdom and love. Spiritualism is a science governed by the law that governs spirits. It is not a set of miracles of God, made under the influence of love or hate, or when God is angry or pleased.

The God of Science abides by law. He performs all his works under the control of law, or is guided by it, and proves his existence by the laws of nature and spirit.

The gods of all other religions are man-made, lawless despots. The only proof that is presented of their existence, is the assertion that they can and have made miracles in violation of the laws of nature and spirit.

The greatest study of the miracle or word god religionists is to get faith, or to increase it in their feelings.

'The greatest study of the scientific religionists is to get knowledge and wisdom.

We often hear of people loving not wisely but too well and that they had too much love and faith, but never that they had too much knowledge and wisdom.

The faith religionists believe, that the best and most innocent of animals, birds and men, must be sacrificed to save the worst of mankind.

The scientific religionists believe that it is necessary to sacrifice the worst of beasts, birds and man to save the best of mankind, to bring about the millenium that is so much desired by the people of earth. They do not think that such a government will be established by the worst of men.

The Christian religion is a summary of all the ancient religions. It contains the principles of all their schemes of salvation and their various plans of worship, to attract the attention of the people. They all begin alike by commands. People must believe, and they can then cure the sick, raise the dead and be saved from all misery here and hereafter. They must have faith and they can remove mountains by a wish. They must love their neighbors as they do themselves, and they will do all duties of life correctly and justly, no matter how unjust their self-love may be.

The scientific religion commenced about six hundred years ago, by discoveries in some of the sciences. They were not considered a religion at the time, only by Christian priests; but little by little discoveries were made. Other sciences, that gave knowledge to the people, were discovered, until the science of spiritualism was established. Then it became known that all these sciences of knowledge formed the basis of a new religion, that was to give joy to all the people of earth. Their only worship is their devotion to get knowledge and wisdom, and learn from them what is best for man to do to avoid pain and misery.

The ancient religions and Christian gods made matter, and then made the heavens and earth, animals and man out of it. Then they made spirits and devils and angels out of it, and all this was done by a word—by their god of words. Ministers and priests have tried to imitate their gods and make all the food and clothing and supply all the wants of mankind by words. The words were plenty but the people starved for the want of food, and died for the necessaries of life. Their faith, their belief, their prayers of priests and people did not stop the famine or stay the pestilence. This shows that words will not produce bread, nor cure diseases, and people must look to other means to obtain the needs of life on earth.

Man was not made to govern the laws of nature and spirit, but these laws were made to govern man. They are his God and they must be his guide. If he would have his wants supplied, man may violate the laws of health and bring on disease. He may violate the laws of peace and bring on war. He may violate the laws that produce good, strong, healthy children, and bring forth weak and sickly ones, who are deformed in body and mind. He may make unjust and unequal laws and a government to enforce them, causing misery, wrongs, conflicts, wounds and death. But the laws of nature and spirit continue just the same. He may make machinery that will chain the lightning, but he cannot destroy the law which governs lightning. It is compliance with nature's god that gives peace, plenty, health and happiness; not faith, not belief, not prayer. The god of nature does not heed such things. But the spirits do, and by them many wonderful things are done, that preachers and priests proclaim as the works of their gods, and the ignorant and superstitious believe them, and are punished by pain and by want.

This makes the god of nature a moral ruler, guided by the laws of justice, to govern mankind. If persons obey the laws of health and peace they have them. If they say they do not know what these laws are, the god of nature is not to blame for that. He has given you intellect and time enough to e arn them. But you have employed your time and talent in useless prayers, instead of learning the truth. You preferred ignorance to knowledge, and you must suffer until you prefer knowledge to ignorance. Guided by these principles, the scientists have put forth the best system of morals ever adopted by mankind, and made the best governments that have ever been established on earth. Their moral principles are the parliamentary laws and rules.

Protestanism is a mixed religion, partly Pagan and Christian, and partly scientific, just calculated to be the medium for people to take, when leaving the faith and sacrificial religions to adopt the scientific. It proclaims the right of private judgment. This mixes a little scientific thought with its ancient superstition and ignorance. When the Christians had control, they used the hangman's rope and fiery faggot to prevent free discussion. For more than a hundred years the infidels and scientists have had about as much to do in shaping the laws, morals and governments of Protestant countries as Christians have. During this time the Protestant countries have gained all their glory, and have dominated the world. Their moral principles have reached all nations, and changed for the better the thoughts and habits of the people. Wherever scientific Protestants go, there are the best and most enlightened people of the earth.

How are we expected to worship so as to be satisfied with faith and belief ? Just as the Christians and other sacrificial religionists do : Count our beads. Bow to our maker. Kneel to our God. Read his holy books. Depend on the priests to save our souls. Pray to God, to Christ, to the Holy Ghost, to the Virgin Mary the mother of God. Do penance and torture the body by priestly orders, to save the soul. Sacrifice the best of animals and man, to save the worst. Repent and ask God in the most piteous supplications to forgive them their sins of commission and omission. Wrestle and agonize with their God, to give them the blessings they ask for. Do anything but get knowledge and wisdom, for these destroy such faith and belief.

How shall we worship to be satisfied with knowledge and wisdom? Our devotions must be of the same kind that scientists apply when they study their special sciences—of thoughtful study and work. We must devote ourselves to obtaining knowledge and using it wisely. Be as devout and earnest, as persevering, peaceful, and determined to find the truth and do right as the best of scientists. Pray to our spirit friends and have them answer our prayers to the best of their ability, and bring us into harmony with the spirits of heaven and the deity that presides over the universe of matter and spirit, decks the heavens with his stars, keeps the sun in its station, the planets in their orbits, and gives the greatest joy to those people who get the most knowledge of his laws and live most wisely in harmony with them. This is the kind of devotion, work and worship, that will satisfy every honest, intelligent person, that the best religion in the world must be based on spiritual knowledge and wisdom.

What is the real importance and value of *Inspiration* as a religious guide? No more important question can be asked in the religious world, because Christianity and all the ancient religions declare inspiration as the only reliable guide for people, and claim it to be better than reason, better than knowledge, better than wisdom, better than all these combined. The scientific religionists declare just the opposite, that the intellect is the only safe guide for people. They wish to heap up knowledge upon knowledge, wisdom upon wisdom, reason upon reason, and make up their judgments from these. to decide what is right and just.

The question is, shall we make our intellect subservient to reason or to inspiration? Shall we throw reason aside as the Christians did during the hundreds of years they had control of the governments, or shall we throw inspiration aside, as is done to-day among the most enlightened people of earth? Here is where the conflict has been raging for more than three hundred years, and the ground on which the battle is being fought to-day. Shall we throw aside intellect and take to inspiration, or throw aside inspiration to be guided by intellect?

To determine this matter, let us inquire into the sources of inspiration. These are impressions, dreams, intuition, clairvoyance, clairaudience, psychology, psychometry, magnetism, communications from spirits and from visions of various kinds. All these, that are claimed to be inspired by God, are asserted to be infallible truth, and the only guide to make peace and good will among the people, and insure them a heavenly home among the blest. Now let us inquire into the sources of knowledge and wisdom. They are obtained by experience, experiments and observations. and finally formulating the facts into sciences. The most important of these is the science of free speech, which the god of words never hinted at, never thought of, although he is made of words and speeches. Wherever this science is complied with, there is intelligence and peace among the people. All the other sciences are made upon its principles of industry, observations and determination to know the truth and abide by it; to know what is right and do it. It has taken ages of hard work and close reasoning to obtain the present knowledge and wisdom, and make the religion of science as it now is. No pains have been spared to make it true and just to all people.

When we turn to the inspirations from the gods, we find them saying: "In six days God made the heavens and earth and all that in them is. The earth was flat, sun, moon and stars went round it," and Christians killed astronomers, because they proved that all their astronomical statements from Genesis to revelations are falsehoods.

Why did the Christians wish to destroy the geologists? Simply because they proved that all the statements of their inspired writers, about the making of the crust of the earth and its animals, its vegetables and its man, were false.

Why did the Christians kill chemists? Simply because they proved that all the inspired chemical statements of their bible were falsehoods. There

were more than the four elements of matter—earth,
air, fire and water.

Why have all religious people killed mediums for
spirit control? Simply because they proved there
was no hell, and that heaven was as natural a place
for spirits as earth was for their bodies, and that the
whole of the inspirations of their bible leads to falsehoods and brutality.

Why have all the most religious people such a
deadly hatred of quiet, independent free-thinkers, and
even kill them now in the most barbarous portions of
catholic and protestant countries? It is simply because they expose the falsehoods of their bible inspirations and the lies of their priests, and tell the truth.

Why have the Christians and Protestants made a
church militant, or fighting church? Simply because
they wish to uphold falsehood, lies, brutality and injustice. There is no other way to uphold the barbar-
ities that are required to maintain such religions, and
the priests and most intelligent people learned this
ages ago, when they founded their religions upon the
falsehoods believed to be true by the ignorant and
superstitious.

Now let us call together the most intelligent of
all these scientists, free-thinkers, mediums, spiritualists and all others that the churches have rejected,
and see if we cannot find among them the stone of
truth and *justice*, that will be exactly fitted to become
the chief head of the corner of the new religious
edifice. Persons who wish to establish the religion of
truth and justice need no church militant, but a fair
hearing, such as parliamentary law affords, and an intelligent people who seek to be just and true.

From these statements the reader will note the
great necessity of a new religion that will be in
harmony with the government and the knowledge of
the people of this age, have all the humanitarian
principles that possess the best of people, and in
every way teach them the importance of being guided
by wisdom in declaring their principles, and making
associations, and working to benefit mankind.

CHAPTER I.

THE SCIENCE OF FREE SPEECH.

This is parliamentary law and the moral basis of the scientific religion. These laws are established upon the moral principles of the equal rights of all people in Religion, Associations, Society and Governments. They secure to every individual, in legislative bodies the same rights; and by principle they secure to every individual in the nation the same rights. They are the best system of laws ever made by man, or by the God believed in by man, to civilize and enlighten the people of any society or nation.

For hundreds of years men have been engaged in legislative bodies in learning what rules and laws they should be guided by, to enable each one of them to have the just rights, in the work that it is their duty, or wish to do. They have made experiment after experiment, and trial after trial, to determine the rules and laws to secure every member of a legislative body his just rights, in manner, action and speech. In this they have set an example for all people to follow in the common affairs of life, if they wish to end civil strife and do justly by all persons of all nations. They teach practical morality, not a theoretical or visionary one. Their demand is that people shall be civil, polite and just in their manners toward each other.

They repudiate the idea, that man should be a law unto himself, and do by others as they would have others do by them. The law of order; can not be made in that way, nor equal rights to free speech. But when a question of right arises in legislatures

and a person is called to order, the point of order is
stated. Then the presiding officer makes a decision.
If that is not satisfactory, an appeal is taken to the
members of the house to determine what is right law
on the subject. There is no question about their loving their neighbor as themselves, or wether they love
anybody, or hate anybody. The only question is,
what is the just law? and majority decides the point
of order, and after a great many decisions makes the
law. Then the law becomes the guide; not love,
not feeling, not conscience, not selfish love, or
unselfish love; but the law of agreement, and so bind-
ing is this law, that it governs the unruly tongues
of the legislators, and if the same equal rights laws
are made to guide all adult people, they will make
similar laws, that will not only govern their tongues,
but all their actions, and make the same order in
general society, that we have now in legislative
bodies.

The making of these laws, is one of the most wonderful works of man that is recorded in history. It
was commenced in the last centuries of the Christian
dark ages, by the great and wealthy men of England;
getting a charter from their king and forming a parliament to secure equal rights by law to the nobles of
that country. This ruling class kept united in all
the vicissitudes of the dark and middle ages of priestly
brutality. Their head men were often killed by the
order of kings or queens. The common people sometimes rebelled, and swept king and parliament out of
existence for a time. But the great men held to their
charter and their rights, and finally triumphed over
kingcraft and priestcraft, ignorance and superstition and proved that the best laws ever made for
man, where made by man. This occured less than
two hundred years ago. Wherever Englishmen go
they carry with them this basic principle of just law,
equal rights, and wherever they plant a colony they
plant the equal rights of man, in place of the equal
rights of nobles ; and these principles soon ripen into
the principle of the equal rights of all its citizens and
the nations, made from such colonies declare that "the
just powers of the government are derived from the

consent of the governed", and the sentiments of equal rights become the principles of the people and governments ; and all are derived from the parliamentary laws that were established by the ruling classes of England under the most oppressive circumstances that ever surrounded a people.

No other nation ever planted such colonies and became the mother of such nations of enlightened people, and no other nation ever made such a just system of laws for its citizens to carry to their colonies, and to other nations and people. Look at the Spanish colonies, and nations made from them. The French colonies, the colonies made by the Germans, Russians and Italians, look the world over, ancient and modern and find if you can, any nation that has equaled the English, in making just governments and an enlightened people.

As they have excelled all other nations in giving just law and knowledge to their people, the question is, how did they do it? What made them do it? Because they had better principles back of their laws, than any other nation, and consequently better laws, and as the basis of their laws was just, all the people have to do, is to follow out the principles and the people will be filled with joy and the nations will be at peace.

Can reformers find in all the world, among all the people better basic-principles to make peace on earth and good will among the people, than the parliamentary laws and principles, to guide them ? A few of these principles were adopted hundreds of years ago, and laws made consistent with them and the people that adopted most of them, are the most enlightened and have the best laws, and the people who refuse to adopt any of them are the most cruel, barbarous, ignorant and superstitious of people in this world. These are the practical results of the two systems and give an unmistakable lesson to guide all, what course to persue, a true religion, a just government and peace among the people of the earth.

CHAPTER II.

ASSOCIATION.

The great question before the American people at this time, is, how shall they associate, to be just to all people ? The answer is, if there is a just government in the world, adopt its laws and principles, if there is not, take the just laws and principles that exist in all governments and add to them all the just ones, that can be conceived by the persons forming the governments and accociations. Every family is a little association under a general government. Unite a number of families and you have a large association. Now, shall all these associations from the family to the state and nation, have the same laws and principles of government ? If they agree, there will be peace and harmony; if not, there will be a constant conflict, it may be war.

1. They must agree to reason together upon the principles of scientific speech, in all their discussions and meetings. This will give all persons the same rights of speech in all the governments from the family to the state and nation. And so far there is now a general harmonious union.

2. The best and most intelligent of husbands and wives agree that they shall have equal rights to life, liberty, property and the pursuit of happiness. This is simply justice, and the declared principles of this government. Yet there is no law of any state or nation that is in accord with this agreement. Here you have a disagreement between the best family laws that the best of men and women make, and the best laws and institutions that best of governments have been willing to make. Notwithstanding it is just, and in agreement with the declared rights of the people, the governments prefer to adopt the laws and bickerings of the worst of husbands and wives, to doing justice, and as they agreed to do when contending for liberty and right.

3. The wages working people have associated together, to have fair living wages for fair work. Shall they have it ? Yes, says every fair-minded man, yet

there is not a law of any state or nation in the world
that will force men to pay it, or even oblige them to
make an investigation to determine what is fair pay
for working people. Here is a perfectly just demand
from every humane person and all wages working
people, that laws be passed to investigate and determine what is fair living wages that should be paid to
working people, for fair work, and the state and
nation having determined what such wages are, they
should pass laws that contracts below such prices
shall be null and void. This will bring harmony among
all the people of these associations who love justice,
and the state and national laws, and make, in this
matter, laws that are in harmony with the just claims
of these associations, and with the profession of the
lawmakers.

4. Working people have associated together to
ask to have the hours of labor so regulated that all
necessary work shall be done, and not so much more,
as to produce a surplus and cause the dismissal of the
workers. TEN HOURS have been tried, and too much
is produced, now the demand is that EIGHT HOURS
shall be tried to determine whether so many hours will
produce all needed supplies. This law is resisted with
venom, by the great majority of employers and executive officers of the state and national governments.
The law of the United States that EIGHT HOURS shall
be a days work, was not allowed to working people,
until after years of agitation; the republican officers
who have been in power for a number of years
long refused to enforce these laws, and the democra-
tic president who vetoed a bill while governor of New
York, that reduced the hours of labor from sixteen
hours per day to twelve for car drivers in New York
City, will hardly be in favor of making the officers
obey the law, or trying the experiment, until working
people, and their friends, unite and demand it at the
BALLOT BOX. Here was an outrageous violation of
laws, and public opinions, by the officers of the
governments, and the animus of the two great parties,
that are contending for supremacy in the government,
is, that they hate the working people and all laws that
favor them, and will do all they can to have them

paid starvation wages, or refuse to pay them anything, until the workers are made insane or partly so, by hard work, poor fare, and insults and inhuman treatment. Then when these poor demented working people rise in mobs and riots, these officers without looking at the cause, can order the soldiers to shoot them down on the spot, and men, women and children are killed and these officers are paid great wages for doing it, and more money is expended in doing this, than would be required, to settle the whole affair quietly, peacefully and justly. But the tax payers have to foot the bills, and the officers are delighted with their large pay and bloody work against insane mobocrats.

When Gov. Rusk of Wisconsin was notified that it was necessary for him to send a military force to put down a mob of rail road working men that were violating the rights of the citizens, he sent to learn the cause of the riots and found it to be, the men had not been paid their dues, and at once, he ordered them to be supplied with provisions that they were made partly insane by not receiving them, and they became quiet, and being assured that justice should be done to them there was no occassion for soldiers to shoot them, and the people were not taxed to pay a military force, to suppress riotous people.

Now let us turn to the works of the governors of Pennsylvania and Ohio who have had frequent occasion to put down the riotous proceedings of working people, when they have been made almost, or quite insane, by want of pay, to enable them to get a comfortable living, sometimes because employers would not pay them what they had agreed to, at other times, from starvation wages. But whatever the cause, the governors were bound to punish them, order soldiers to shoot them if necessary, to make them submit to be starved peacefully, or worked and starved to death, amidst plenty and to spare. The question to tax payers and all peace, loving citizens is: Will you join the working men's party as much as Gov. Rusk has, and have peace, or join those who are opposed to working people having their just dues, and have taxations, starvation and mobs as the governors of Pennsylvania and Ohio have. If you refuse to deal justly with the working people now, you will be taxed heavily for your injustice and your children and children's children will raise monuments in honor of the working people you starved and shot. The same as John Brown is now honored because he gave his life to free the slaves.

5. Marriages and divorces shall be civil contracts and their settlements, made upon the scientific principles that produce the best children and make the most harmonious, happy and healthy people.

The God of nature made the laws of attraction and repulsion in the marriage relation, and it is the duty of man to make laws that are in harmony with them. If they are not, there will be constant conflict, as is now seen in most of the families that the priests say God has joined together, and let no man put asunder. If God has done that, he has united people to produce miserable children, and live in inharmonious, unhappy and unhealthy conditions. There is no proof that any such God exists, except such as priests have made and superstitious and deluded people worship. We ask the governments of the state and nation to pass laws, that are in harmony with the God of nature, that makes all the natural children, and agrees with the natural man and woman. When a Mrs. Clark uttered the sentiment in the Wisconsin State Agricultural Association at the meeting held at Madison in the spring of 1885: "That the best stock raised on the farm were the children", she told a great truth and now what is wanted, is for people to have the right, by law, to so unite that they can raise the very best of this best stock, and this must be, before the governments are in harmony with the God of nature, and with the most thoughtful people in the world.

6. Only such persons should be admitted to the association as members, who are in entire sympathy with its objects and aims, and profess a willingness to do the work required of them, to become useful to the association, and it may be they should not become members until they had proved their usefulness by

years of work in the association. One of the greatest difficulties in forming a just association that contains a number of families is to get suitable, faithful members who will work together harmoniously and profitably; but the greatest of all difficulties, is that there are no laws of the states or nation, except parliamentary laws, that will allow people to do right by each other in all the affairs of life, and such laws can not be made until men and women have equal rights by law. Now, while persons are allowed to receive great incomes that are not taxed extra, that is by a graduated income tax, while individuals and corporations can hold large tracts of land, therefore such great landed estates and incomes should be taxed out of existence.

And if the land is not wanted for settlement by individuals to belong to the government or state, because justice cannot be done to individuals while any one of these laws exist and are enforced. They divert the earnings of the working people from their just uses, to the wealthy, who spend them in indolence and debauchery; or in instigating riots and war, to prevent the people from enjoying the fruits of their labor, and to establish despotisms where their wealth will allow them to rule with despotic sway. It is a great curse to the rich and poor; in civilized society, it makes the rich forget that a God of justice rules, and makes the poor curse the God that made them, and the people who instituted the laws that curse them. These are the teachings of history.

Many more laws might be cited to show that a just association can not be formed, and have it legal, and it is the duty of people to make their associations, upon just principles whether lawful or unlawful, and live as near to the just principles as the law and public opinion will allow, and try to induce the people to make the laws of justice that will make it legal to do right. There are three laws that contain the just general principles to guide people in making the laws of justice:

1. We adopt the science of free speech. This gives equal rights to all members in meetings for the discussion and consideration of all subjects.

2. We adopt the scientific principles of a just government. These give all citizens the same rights to life, liberty, property and the pursuit of happiness.

3. We adopt as the first and most important law under these general principles, that wages-working persons shall have just compensation for their labor, and this shall be determined by the cost of living. Always taking into consideration that these laborers must be paid more than just sufficient for their support, to enable the economical to lay up livings for a time of sickness, or when out of work. All history proves that the destruction of the best governments have been caused by injustice to the poor laborers, making slaves of them by law, or by starvation wages. Then the rulers have gone to fighting, to control the spoils of office and to rule or ruin the governments. If these three principles are made into the laws of the land, there can hardly be any oppression that the people would not soon check. If people have free speech, and equal rights, and the working people can not be oppressed in their wages, it will make an independent people, who will right all the wrongs of associations and governments very soon.

The first great object in making an association based upon scientific principles, is to show people that they can live better, healthier and happier in that way, than by any other system. The second great object is to set before all people, an example to guide in establishing their scientific religions and political governments, that are best fitted to nature, the natural earth, the natural man, and the natural God.

The great difficulty, in forming associations, has been, that working people were treated as infants, not to be trusted with their own earnings, but require guardians. The Shakers take this view in practice in their associations. The Oneida communists had the same ideas in a less degree. The American socialists practiced on the same plan. A scientific association must be formed upon the theory that every adult man or woman who is admitted as a partner in the association, is capable of managing their earnings and property and there should be a settlement every year, (at least one), and every partner should receive their share of the net profits of the association, to do as they please with it. We will suppose farming to be the business of the association. The first thing to be done is to get the funds to pay for the land, then buy and stock it, so as to begin its cultivation, when the people can be found that can live and work together profitably. The land is our church, the workers of it are the worshipers and the law God that produces the growth of the vegetables and animals, guides them to do the best work, that will produce the best of earthly products, to make man happy and make harmony and peace among the people and will cause people to live in agreement with their God; and his natural law will be their natural law, and his products shall be theirs, and his spirits shall be the peoples, spirits and these angels of God and spirits of mankind shall be the advisers of these working people in all the affairs of life, and then it will be known that the God that makes the best angels of heaven, makes the best products of earth, and he who makes the laws for the spirits of heaven, makes the laws for the people of earth, and all are under one set of divine laws and the same virtues that save people on earth will save them in heaven, and the same justice that gives people their rights on earth, will give them their rights in heaven, and the same love that will make a mother give up her life for her child on earth, will make her devote her life in heaven to comfort and shield her child from harm.

There is no hope that any persons can be good associationists, unless they adopt the principle that the best teachers are the best and most intelligent workers, doing the most important work to support the people and make them most comfortable. Word worshipers who take the highest positions in the past religions, will take the lowest in this, because they have been more often false and frauds, than just and true. People are wanted that are willing to go into partnership with the land they cultivate and give the land a fair part of the products to keep it in good condition and to pay the taxes on it, and make such improvements as will cause it to be in better heart every year it is under their care, and if there is a surplus above all the necessities of the land and stock, the surplus should be used to buy more land to enlarge the association or to make new associations, to be conducted on the best plans that can be devised by knowledge, experience and wisdom.

When we take into consideration the strength, duties and obligations of man and woman that natural law imposes on them, we see how difficult it is for a husband and wife to be so harmoniously united that the wife will not become the slave of her husband and children and live a wretched life of toil and suffering, and often both of them, and become partial slaves to hired help, or the hirelings become their slaves. To remedy this condition of life, associations should be formed, where each person can do their duty and not be overtaxed by husband, wife, children or hired help. To make such an association a living, peaceful harmonial success, requires a great amount of knowledge, experience and wisdom Human nature is so various and complicated by needs and wants, mistakes and ambition that it takes a long time for people to learn what is good hate and what is bad hate, what is good love and what is bad, what is good selfishness and what is bad, what is good practical life and what is bad, and how to take good care of themselves, to enable them to take good care of others.

Until they have been educated in all these things and are taught that they are responsible beings and must take the responsibilities of life, in associations, or in general society, they are not prepared to enter associations as full partners, but only as pupils, and receive only such share of the net profits as belong to students and apprentices. When this is done we have equal rights principles as the basic rules of families and associations for a foundation for a just republican religion and government.

CHAPTER III.

RELIGION.

The word religion, is derived from the Latin *religio*, and this is said to be derived from *relegere*, (to reconsider), and also from *religare*, (to bind fast). In the widest sense of the word, it comprehends all forms of faith and acts of worship. Its theological meaning is: To bind and rebind people to their God. Practically, in all the great religions, it has been the rule of the priests in the name of God. Scientifically it means: That the laws of nature bind and rebind all people to the God of nature, and they cannot help themselves. The Law-God of nature, rules man, and man, to be in agreement with this God, must make laws that are in harmony with man's necessities and nature's laws. Man, being forced to obey the laws of nature, must have the moral right to do so, in their religious associations, and they must be in harmony with the material associations that proclaim these rights. These are based on scientific free speech, equal rights and good living wages to laborers.

Having adopted this moral code and these moral principles, that are the wordly basis of the true religion, the next great object is to adopt the true worship of the true God that rules the heavens and the earth, by the fixed and unalterable laws of nature. He made the earth for man to cultivate foolishly, and be in want; or wisely and have abundance. He gives men minds to acquire knowledge and wisdom, that will bring them into harmony with the law God of nature; or, they can refuse to get knowledge and wander after other gods, and ignorantly and foolishly ask them to protect their persons from the penalties of ignorance and folly, and to turn stones into bread to keep them from starving, and water into wine, that they may get drunk and forget their troubles; but the wise religious people will calculate to get their bread from grain raised under the natural laws, and never drink wine to get drunk.

The first great duty of the scientific religious, is to get knowledge and wisdom ; the second, to do all work according to their greatest knowledge and highest wisdom. This is the most sacred worship ever offered to a deity, and has produced the most wonderful blessings ever showered upon a people.

In getting this knowledge of earthly matters, the scientists have relied upon experience and observations. In getting a knowledge of the spiritual heavens, they have relied upon the information of spirits through the mediums—brought out by modern Spiritualism—and these have been consulted upon all earthly subjects, with great benefit to the persons consulting them.

From these statements it is plain to see the difference between the ancient religions and the scientific Christianity is founded on faith obtained from ancient sacred books ; the words are sacred, whether true or false, and the falsehoods which they convey to the reader, are as sacred as their truths, and they are read with the same solemn, impressive air, as those that are true. The scientists allow nothing to be sacred but truth and justice, tempered with mercy. It must be proved true and just before it becomes sacred. The Christians' greatest study is to increase their faith and love in their feelings ; the scientific religionists' greatest study is to get knowledge and wisdom, that will enable them to form just judgments. The Christians make knowledge subject to faith, and wisdom subject to love ; the scientific religionists make faith subject to knowledge, and love subject to wisdom. We often hear of people loving not wisely but too well, and that they had too much love and faith, but never that they had too much wisdom and knowledge.

The Christian religion is a sacrificial religion, based upon the horrible principle that the best man was murdered to save the worst, and it proclaims all the best and worst principles of all the sacrificial religions. These good and bad principles are so ingeniously put together as to deceive a great many of the best of people, and are the delight of the greatest of deceivers and the power of popes, cardinals and other clergy. Their bible was made and proclaimed holy, for that purpose, by a set of lying priests. Moshiem says all would lie—not an exception is made, and he is one of the most reliable of Christian writers. The religious scientists reject all such books as authority to establish any truth or justice, and reconsider the statements with the greatest care. This has caused the Christians to murder them as long as they could keep up that barbarism, and to slander them for telling the truth, even to this day.

From this history of Christianity and Christians, the conclusion is reached, that the more true and just the statements of reformers are, the more their enemies will persecute and slander them. As an example, we will turn to the history of Thomas Paine. He was one of the purest and noblest men that ever lived on earth. His life was devoted to doing good to mankind. He proclaimed his religious opinions, and it seems no better were ever uttered, or can be. He believed in one God, and no more. So do the Christians, but they divide him into three pieces, and Paine did not, and they abused him for not doing their bidding, in the most slanderous manner. The world was his country; heaven was the Christians' country. It would seem that these countries were far enough apart, so that they need not quarrel about the possession, but the Christians invaded the world, proving that they were not honest in their declaration, and meant to lie and deceive the people, and they said all manner of evil of Paine, and persecuted him as much as the times would permit, because he said this was a blessed world. His religion was to do good. The Christian religion was to do Christ. Here is the point where Christian spite and vengeance showed itself in the most cruel manner. For more than a hundred years they have traduced him, and lied about him, because he said virtue would save the people. It seems as though the Christians' total depravity or incarnate devil had entered them, to make them say all manner of evil of him since his death, as they have, and continue it yet. He hoped for eternal life; so do the Christians; yet nothing abates the Christian vengeance, because he did not approve the action of the priests, who were known to be the worst class of learned people in the world, and always had been. He simply told the truth about them.

Here we have a little sketch of the religions of one of the greatest and best men that ever lived ; a hero of our revolution and of the French revolution of 1789 ; a man who always contended for the just rights of the people wherever he was, on the Eastern or Western continents or the islands of the sea ; a man whose character for truth, honesty, intelligence, virtue and bravery, was never excelled. If such a man is persecuted and reviled for telling the truth and proclaiming as good a religion as was ever uttered by man, what can ordinary men or women expect but to lose their lives by Christian malice if they proclaim the true religion, and get the people to combine together to put it in practice ?

Let the result be what it may ; we have the example of Thomas Paine to be guided by. He adopted the best principles he knew, and was guided by them to the best of his ability. We must adopt the best we know and can agree upon, and live by them as near as it is possible in this age. The religion that was fastened upon the world by a set of lying priests in the 4th century, controls the making of laws, so that truth is not allowed to be told by infidels in courts of justice and equity, and is considered infamous slanders when told out of court, will prevent people from living just lives, as long as they are the law of the land. But let us claim the right to make right laws and live by them as best we can, until the people finally declare that no law on the statute book shall be interpreted so as to prevent people from doing right and speaking the truth, in this country, in court or out of it.

From these statements it is seen that there can be no agreement between persons believing in these different religions. One says the greatest salvation comes from the blood of the lamb ; the other says the greatest salvation comes from the best work of the most intelligent people. The highest civilization of to-day is based upon the principle of punishing the guilty to save the innocent, and there is not, nor ever was, any people that said that the killing of the innocent, to save the guilty, was the best way of salvation to be adopted, except lying priests or ignorant and fanatical religionists. It is too ridiculous and false to be believed by any but the ignorant and superstitious. If any one will look into the secret history of its adoption by the Christians, they will find, that the priests calculated that the more false and absurd the doctrine they could make people believe, the easier it would be to make them obey their orders, and this, with the trinity, and that faith would remove mountains, and belief will raise the dead, and prayers will stay the pestilence and feed the famishing, better than cleanliness and work, were some of the falsehoods employed by priests to make the ignorance of the people the bliss of the priests, and their superstitions to be the guiding star of their hopes to get earthly riches and honors and heavenly bliss. In this they adopted the worst doctrines that they could find in the archives of Rome, where all kinds of religion were represented, because they found the worst doctrines caused the most powerful priesthoods, and the truer the doctrines, the less important the priests, and it may be prophesied with entire certainty, that when the true religion is adopted by the people, this worst class of learned people the world has ever seen, will disappear from the earth—never to return.

Protestantism is a mixed religion ; partly Christian and partly scientific; just fitted to be the medium for people to take when leaving the sacrificial religion to adopt the scientific. It proclaims the right of private judgment and, at the same time, the words of their God to be infallible truth that must not be disputed. This would seem to stop disputes and arguments on religious subjects. But this was far from the facts. The words of their God's Holy Bible were made to have two meanings; one material, the other spiritual. This enabled the believers to dispute and wrangle about the meaning of words and sentences. There was very little argument used by them for the first hundred years after the reformation. The leaders in this reform used the power of persecution, confiscation, the dungeon and the faggot, to stop arguments on that subject or any other that they thought hinged upon it, and it took about another hundred years before the Christian Protestants were so far reconciled to the right, as to allow people to use it fairly without trying to stop it by the hangman's rope. Since that time, which is more than a hundred years, the scientists have had nearly as much to do in shaping the morals of the people and the laws of Protestant governments as Christians have. During this time, these governments have gained all their glory and dominated the world. Their moral principles have reached all people and changed the thoughts and habits of the people for the better. Any one can see how slow has been the progress from the last end of the middle ages to the present enlightened age ; and further, they can see wherever Christianity goes, there are taught the principles that made the horrors of the dark and middle ages, and wherever the Protestant Christians go, they teach the same doctrines, modified by a restricted free thought. But wherever scientific Protestantism goes, there are the most enlightened and best people of the earth, with the best religious institutions.

From the experience gained in the last six hundred years beginning with the most ignorant people of any in Europe, made so by Christianity, it is easy to see what educated the people. Christianity is just the same as it was then, the same bible, the same worship, the same creeds, the same doctrines and priests acting in the same part, and doing just as they had been for the seven hundred years previously, that had produced the ignorance, superstition and barbarism of the people at that time. Then the people began to get knowledge, the power of the priests began to decay, they began to be guided by the ways of wisdom more, and less by the various wilds of love, until now, when wisdoms ways, are put in practice more than ever before, and love is put down as a fickle jade, that leads to ruin more than to goodness and virtue, the people mistrust the priests who are the greatest of lovers, and the teachers that love are the best guide for people, more than ever before, as they have learned in the past, that thirteen and a half per cent of them have proved criminals and they have every reason to believe they are no better now than they have been. The religion that has been growing for hundreds of years, and is still growing in the minds of the people, is the religion of thought, the religion of ideas, the religion of knowledge, capped and cemented together by wisdom, which proclaims that justice shall be done, tempered with mercy. This is the only compromise that it can make to the ignorant, the superstitious and the wilfully wicked criminals, and teachers of false doctrines, that make the people malicious criminals, as priests have in past times. The time has come when the religion of science, which is wisdom, must be formulated and put in practice more than ever before, because the people have become so intelligent as to call for it, and the teachers of the new religion must put its principles and theories into the most practical form possible, to be up with the demands of the age, upon them. They must make a religion that will accept new ideas, and be as progressive as other sciences, and not stand alone as Christianity does, a monument of the dark ages, but its monument should be in harmony with the times and ready to receive all truth that is discovered in coming ages. — Why are religious people so divided as all religions are based on spiritualism. The Buddhists turn from Spiritualism and worship Buddha their God, as more true than truth, more just than justice, more virtuous than virtue, more wise than wisdom, more good than goodness, more knowing than knowledge, and better to follow, than the best in all space, and all time. The followers of Confucius and all the Pagan Asiatic man Gods, word Gods and spirit Gods, worship them because of this belief. The Jews followed their spirit God, Jehovah, because he was better than justice. The Greeks and Romans followed their Gods, Jupiters and others because they were stronger than truth and better than justice, and more peaceful than the laws of nature. All these religionists left spiritualism and followed some imaginary God and went to killing each other, instead of reasoning together. The Christians took the best and worst of all these religions and made their Christ and Christianity. They left Spiritualism and made a man God, word God and spirit God and then went to killing those who did not worship their one-three God. They condemned reason, and that left them nothing but beastly fighting to settle disputes. The Swedenborgians left Spiritualism and followed Swedenborg. The Mohammedans left spiritualism and worshiped Mohammed. The Mormons left spiritualism and followed Joe Smith. All these religionists have left spiritualism, truth and humanity to follow some man of God that they thought stronger and better, and they have shed rivers of blood to establish it, but have never let in reason to prove it, and with all the facts of knowledge, to settle the disputes. Now come Spiritualists with their religion of reason. They stand by Spiritualism as a great spiritual fact. It joins with truth, justice and humanity and declares that each and every one of these is greater, and more powerful than all the prophets, Gods, Christs and saviours, that the world has ever seen. Spiritualism is more spiritual, truth is more true, justice is more just, humanity is more humane, than any or all the Gods, saviours, Christs and prophets, that ever existed. The law of nature is their God, the spirits of heaven are their advisers, and reasonable conclusion, their aim, knowledge and wisdom their object to guide them to humane principles. They agree with the principles of a just government. All these subjects will be considered at the Mount Pleasant Park Camp Meeting in August, by those who wish it, there by the side of the great father of waters, near the center of the continent of North America, we will declare the truest religion and the best government ever uttered by man or his God.

Chapter IV.

GOVERNMENT.

Governments derive their just powers from the consent of the governed. This is a true brilliant statement that flashed on the world of mankind from the minds of some of the most advanced thinkers, more than a hundred years ago, and has been read and quoted as an inspirational and reasonable truth ever since, yet has never been put into law practically, except in parliamentary laws, which I denominate the science of free speech. Our lawmakers adopt thisscience to keep them in order, when discussing the questions arising among them in making laws. They have made laws that gave people equal rights to talk in their meetings, but never that gave them equal rights in their work as citizens. That is, equal rights to life, liberty, property and the pursuit of happiness. If they adopt such a law they will be in harmony, so far, with the best principles that a husband and wife can adopt, and the best that larger associations can agree upon, and until such a law is passed they are in harmony with the worst principles that control husbands and wives, and the worst principles that people adopt in larger associations, because the law that compels the wife to be subject to the husband, or the husband be subject to the wife, or one that makes the wife give her earnings to the husband and deprives her of the necessaries of life, is just as much a thief, as is the sneak thief that steals her earnings.

The next great work of the government is to make laws that will give wages working people FAIR LIVING PAY FOR FAIR WORK. For more than eighty years after the people of this country declared their independence, the government upheld slavery, and in that time they raised up the most brutal set of masters and their toadies, that ever cursed a nation. Their plan was to give the slaves the poorest fare that it was possible for them to live on and work, and when the work was not satisfactory, they were brutally punished, it may be whipped, until their backs were cut by the lash to a jelly and then washed with salt and water ; this was all the pay they were allowed, for their faithful work. To support this system, the owners of these slaves made war on the government, and now look at the cost of whipping them and freeing the slaves. Behold our brothers starving in Libby and Andersonville and tortured by these brutes in the most excruciating manner that they had learned by theory and practice in a life time. All this came upon our intelligent faithful soldiers and citizens, because we had allowed men and women to be held as slaves, and worked, starved and tortured to death. When it came to war, our most faithful Union citizens were starved and tortured to death. This was the most diabolical penalty that the people of this country had to pay, for permitting persons to own and punish the working classes. Now we are raising up another, just such a set of brutal gentlemen and ladies and their bulldozing assistants, who are in favor of forcing laborers to work at starvation wages, and a great majority of the rulers of the states and nation, agree to use their military power, and shoot the workmen who rebel against being worked and starved to death, and are engaged in riotous acts because made partly insane, by want and insults. Public opinion does not allow them to be burned at the stake and tortured and murdered as the slaves were, but there is no law to prevent riotous workmen from being used as rebellious slaves were, and soon these gentlemen and ladies will override · public opinion and introduce tortures of the most painful sort to prevent workmen from demanding their just rights. unless the people rise in their might and declare that wages working people shall have good living pay for their work.

If any one doubts these statements about pay for work, let them take a case into any of the courts of justice or equity ; say a railroad worker or miner, who is receiving 65 cents a day, and prove that it costs at least $1.00 to live anything like comfortable a day, and that a little more should be allowed to enable the economical to lay by for a rainy day. The court will show the contract that their wages were to be less. Yes, that is true, says the worker, but it's a swindle ;

I cannot live on it. Now, what I want, is fair living pay for my fair work, and I declare that contract is not as sacred as justice. I want sufficient pay to keep soul and body together, and this will not do it, and the Court will dismiss the case and turn the workman out of court before he had really time to state his case. Perhaps he will be informed that workingmen have no rights that gentlemen employers are obliged to respect, or that these gentlemen have the divine rights of kings to starve working people, or under any consideration, the contract is more sacred than justice.

The judges will not institute a commission to en-quire into the facts and justice of the case, as did Gov. Rusk of Wisconsin as referred to in my chapter on association, but will follow the guide of the gover-nors of Ohio and Pennsylvania, and have the workers shot instead of paid. Some swindling contracts are annulled, but not those that swindle wages workers. It seems the determination of most of the rulers of the state and nation, to tax people to support monopolists now, as it was anterior to the rebellion to support the slave holders. The same arguments are used in each case, that they have the entire right to get the most work they can, out of workers at the least cost. This state of things can not last long, before gentlemen will begin to threaten senators and representatives and finally knock them down in their seats as Sumner was by Preston S. Brooks, if they are as persistent for workmen as he was for the slaves. Then in defence of their brutality they will say of the senators and representatives the same that Senator Butler of South Carolina said of Sumner, that they never had been in good society, although they may have been in the best society in the Northern states and Europe as Sumner had ; but he had never been much in the society of gentlemen in the Southern states, who made laws to whip women and make them submit to the most dis-graceful acts, and who had sworn allegiance to the United States government and boasted of violating their solemn oaths, and who were accustomed to fight duels to defend their honor when they had no moral honor to defend, and they will send hundreds of canes to the gentleman brute who will do the deed as they did to Brooks ; then will come a bloody Kansas to end in another war, where these gentlemen and ladies will unite again to make Andersonville for those who expose the cause of the wages working people, for it must be remembered that the men who send to foreign countries and make contracts with workers there, for them to come to this country and work at starvation wages and insist that such workmen as are living here shall take such pay or be turned off, to make room for these deceived foreigners, and the officers of the state or nation that approve of the man who vetoed the bill to reduce the car driver's time for a days work from sixteen hours per day to twelve hours will finally do any cruelty to oppress wages working people. The approving of such vetoes means that the persons do not care for the safety of the passengers, or the lives of the drivers. They are determined to have despotic power and the barbarism that it inflicts. When these gentlemen are supported by the military and naval officers, wo refuse the eight hour law, you can see how little respect they have for law, public opinion or humanity, when they have power to commit cruelties on wages working people.

The history of the world, and of this country shows that the abuse of the working people destroys the best governments, it made hells in place of the most enlightened governments of Greece, Rome and the Southern states of this union, as an eminent officer of our union is reported to say "war is hell". Abuse of working people makes constant war ; as Thomas Jefferson had said "there is constant war between master and slave" and this can not continue many years, without making war among the masters and their toadies against the working people. It is useless to expect any different result of the trial in this Union. Many times workingmen strike on wrong principles, and this will always be the case until just laws are made to guide them. When courts are authorized to send out commissioners to determine the cost of living, and legislatures send out committees to report what fair living wages must be, to be fair to the laborer, and the reports of committees of societies of laboring people are received as assistance to forming just estimates, and laws passed that governors and presidents are forbid to send soldiers to shoot down strikers, until their cause has been examined, and decided that their claim is unjust, and their riotous doings unjust. Judging from past experience it will be vastly more just to consider rioters innocent until they are proved guilty by a court of equity on the above plan, than to assume that the employers are innocent on the plan that has been adopted in the past.

Look at the South. The employers have formed mob societies, to govern the working people and take control of the governments, and these mobs and governments have been justified by the republicans and democrats and their governments sanctioned by the states and nation, and yet there never have been mobs of working people that where so cruel and bloodthirsty as these employers have been ; and they have not been tried for their murders, but justified and honored by giving them the most important offices. All this has been done, since these employers had been whipped back into the Union, by its military power and have utterly refused to obey the civil power and now have the control of the government. The question before the American people has been for a number of years and is now, shall the military power of the Union govern the Southern states, or shall these mobs govern them ? The question has been settled by the two governing parties, that they prefer the mobs of gentlemen, to the military rule of the Union, which is under the control of the civil power. Republicans may deny this statement, but they had the full power, and allowed mob representatives and senators to take their seats in Congress, and finally they and their copperhead friends in the North have got the control.

Now the question is : what is the bottom cause of the trouble between the North and South ? It is that the North gives every child a chance to get a common school education ; the South has utterly refused to give all the children that chance. The southern plan formerly was to strip female teachers, tar and feather them, and maltreat male teachers, tar and feather them; many of them were murdered. The same hatred is manifested now, as formerly, and school houses are burned and teachers driven off. All the hatred of the Southerners of Northern people has its foundation because they are instructors and will cause the poor whites and blacks to think for themselves. This is proved by their acts to southern instructors as well; no matter who it is that instructs these poor people, they hate them, with all the vengeane of demons. If any one has any doubts about this, let them go on the plantations and commence schools, to faithfully instruct the children. During the war and for a few years after, teachers were permitted to instruct the people, but the statistics from 1870 to 1880, since mob-rule governed these states, show that the people are falling back into their old time ignorance; this makes these states the Russia of America. Ignorance will make a despotism as well in the frigid North as in the torrid South. It is not the hot blood of the South that makes despotism, nor the cool blood of Russia, but the ignorance of the people.

What can be done to unite these people and have a harmonious government ? Make the North 'give up her common school educational institutions, or make the South establish as good common schools for all their children, and see that they are as well educated as northern children are. The first plan will carry the people back to the barbarism of ignorance, if it can be executed, the second will carry the whole country forward to the highest degree of civilization and enlightenment if it can be done. To put this matter at rest and have the representatives and senators show their hands on this subject ; let us send to them for their adoption the following resolution :

" *Resolved*, That every state be required to see that every child has a fair opportunity to learn to read, write and cipher." If they refuse or neglect to do this, they shall be deprived of a representation in Congress, because we know by experience that the rulers in such states mean to destroy this republic and deprive the people of their just rights. Formerly, when they divided the union, they went out of

Congress of their own choice; after this, it is best for the intelligent union people to have their choice.

For the life of this republic rests upon the intelligence of the people, and all states and territories that do not provide schools to give such intelligence to all, we may conclude, are opposed to a just republic, and they should be taxed by the union as all other people tax themselves. These enemies should not be allowed to go untaxed, who have taxable property. The citizens of this republic who are its enemies, who take every opportunity to traduce it and make war upon it, should not be used better than good loyal citizens. The statistics of 1880 show that more than half the people of South Carolina were too ignorant to read and write, and it is well known that this state was the head and front of the rebellion. These statistics further show that nearly half the population of the rest of the states lately in rebellion, were in the same state of ignorance. The question is: Shall the people tax these rebels to educate the people, or let them go untaxed and make a rebellion, and then tax them to put it down as all are taxed? Those persons who oppose taxing the property holders to educate all children, are in favor of war, with its horrors of pestilence and famine, and the torturing of soldiers and prisoners by inhuman officers When all the people are educated alike in this union there will be harmony among them on this most important matter.

The next subject to harmonize the people on, is, the making of laws to regulate the wealth of the country, so that there can not be a useless set of rich do-nothings and a poor set of drones cast upon the country. The object is to build up the great middle class and make it as large as possible and have as few of the very rich and begging poor as can be justified by the best laws that the best of people can make. Such laws as will prevent people from becoming so rich as to forget their duty and their God; or being so poor as to curse the country they live in, and the God that made them. The best way yet devised is by a judicious system of taxes upon incomes and upon great landed estates, so great on land as to finally have the real income go to the cultivators. In all these taxes the United States should have control and make them uniform throughout the union. In all common taxes the states should have control and make them as equal and just as possible.

The salaries of the officers of this government should be consistent with the incomes of the people they represent, the same as the salaries of the rulers of England were made consistent with the lords of England. They were the support of the crown, and it was their plan to make the wearer of that crown have a place superior to any other place in the kingdom, and make it continue during the life of the king or queen. In this government, the president is a representative of all the men citizens of the country, and his salary should be consistent with their incomes and their condition in life. Very few of the presidents have had economy enough to save from their salaries sufficient to support them, after they were retired to private life. This has forced the government to give them pensions and subsidies to prevent them from being paupers in the poor houses of the country. Instead of the great salaries now paid to the president and other great officials, three-fourths of it should be reserved for pauper officials to make them homes, like the soldiers' homes. They need not be under military control, unless that kind of despotism is deemed necessary to keep them in order, as it is with the old crippled soldiers in their homes. The idea is to have good civil homes for all these heroes of peace and war, and not have them begging congress to make gift appropriations for their support.

Of all the most infamous laws ever made to rule a home, the despotic military laws adopted by congress to govern poor old crippled soldiers, in their soldiers' homes, are the worst. These soldiers fought and established the right to have homes governed by civil law, yet congress does not make such homes for them, but puts them under despotic military laws and military incivility, for there is no civility required by these laws of officers to soldiers. It is an insult to these officers, for these disabled veterans to respectfully state their grievances when an officer makes a command; it is talking back, and the poor old cripple must be sent to the guard house for it. It is a command to be obeyed, not a request to be civilly considered, and under tyrants it is the concentration of barbarism, torture and murder. From these insults and cruelties, these old crippled men should be relieved by an act of congress and none should be condemned to military rule until proved guilty of violating some civil law and sentenced by a civil magistrate, after a fair trial. Without this condemnation, it is one of the most dastardly deeds ever committed by a legislative body upon the heroes that saved liberty to their people. I have not space to say more here, but will refer the reader to a pamphlet issued by Geo. M. Hare, entitled "Mysteries and Miseries"; his address is Oshkosh, Wis. He was an inmate of the homes at Dayton, Ohio, and Milwaukee, Wis., for some years and gives a clear statement of the insults, sufferings and punishments inflicted on innocent old heroes by military despots. There are great numbers of people, that join in requesting the governors and legislatures of each and every state, to do all they can to stop the military law, from being the rule to govern in these homes, and we petition the president and congress of the United States to put these homes under civil law. Make them the homes of the free, in the land of the brave.

As the various denominations of Christians have their chaplains appointed to visit and console their church members, I would ask one to be appointed to that office for the Spiritualists and free religionists, as many of them say they are starving for spiritual food and the consolations of the Spiritualists gospel. Dr. Juliet H. Severance has been named as a proper person to fill that office.

The office of president of the United States of America should be abolished, it has more duties to fulfill than any man can do, only as a despot. He can know next to nothing of the capacity of the persons he appoints to office, only in exceptional cases; the secretary should have the appointing power, then we would have warriors at the head of the war department, statesmen at the head of the state department, financiers at the head of treasury department and postmasters at the head of the post office department, if the people wanted to have such persons as their officers.

Now we have peace men for presidents in time of war, like Madison and Lincoln and these do very well, but when the wars are over, we have warriors for presidents in time of peace, like Jackson and Grant, and they make the most disgraceful state appointments ever made. One had his kitchen cabinet and the other his whiskey rings, Indian rings and they quarrelled with the best statesmen of their time like Webster and Clay, and Sumner and Fenton. All they wanted was the power of a Cæsar, a Cromwell, or a Bonaparte, to silence all statesmen who differed with them.

Gen. B. F. Butler may not have been the greatest military commander of modern times, but his record is fair in that regard; but as a statesman general, he has no superior in the annals of history. He quietly submitted to the insults of commanders who knew nothing of statesmanship, either of economy, civil government, financial principles or of the character of the men required to manage the monetary business of the country.

The present president had the worst reputation of any man ever elected to that office. The hope is that he will be like one of old, who to get office was so wicked that the people were sorry he was ever born, but he made such a good ruler that all the people mourned at his death.

ELECTIONS.

There should be two important elections each year. One in the spring to elect local officers, and one in the fall to elect state and national officers. The days appointed for elections should be holidays by state and national laws. Many persons oppose these frequent and important elections. But such should remember that the price of liberty is eternal vigilance, even if they had a whole week of holidays twice a year at election, it would not cost the people as much as it would be worth to them. One year of despotism would cost the people more, than such elections would cost them in a hundred years. All officers should be elected by the men and women voters, that is consistent with a just republic.

MONEY AND CURRENCY.

The United States have entire control of the monetary system of the country. They make and unmake money. If the rulers wish to put down speculation in money, they will see to it that at all centres of trade, money bears the same interest at all times. If the rulers wish to have people speculate in money, they will make it cheap or dear at the bidding of speculators.

CRIMINALS AND INSANE.

All criminals should be treated as insane, and be subjected to the discipline that is required to keep them from harming other people, and teach them their duties in life.

SHALL THE CAPITOL BE REMOVED.

The capitol has been removed many times and there never was a time when there were so many good reasons for its removal as now. 1. It is in one corner of the Union. 2. It is in the rebel corner, where the people hate the government. 3. It is an unhealthy location. 4. Our best men should not be forced to live in these malarial, pestilential districts, among a people made ignorant by state laws and be subjected to rebel platitudes, to make laws for the whole people of this Union. They should be placed in a healthy country, among an intelligent, Union loving people, where the pure air of the North rolls over the rich prairies, near the great father of waters, where it touches the shores of the state of Wisconsin. When the capitol of the Union is placed in such a salubrious climate, among such an intelligent people, it will be a sign that a just republic will last as long as the continent of North America exists as a part of the earth's surface. Let all the people who wish for a good government contend for a good healthy climate for the location of their capitol. Let us talk that over at the great Central Camp Meeting at Mount Pleasant Park, Iowa, at its meeting in August, and learn if attention can be called to the subject in such a manner, as to have representatives from all parts of this continent, who will proclaim that a just government must have its capitol among an intelligent people, in a healthy climate, near the center of their country.

DEMANDS OF THE WOMAN'S RIGHTS PARTY.

"We demand equality with man in all rights, privileges and responsibilities; and that a XVI. amendment to the constitution be framed, guaranteeing to woman protection in the exercise of the right of franchise."

THE DEMANDS OF THE LABOR PARTY,

as presented by the preamble and declaration of principles of the Knights of Labor of America:

The alarming development and agressiveness of great capitalists and corporations, unless checked, will inevitably lead to the pauperization and hopeless degradation of the toiling masses.

It is imperative, if we desire to enjoy the full blessings of life, that a check be placed upon unjust accumulation, and the power for evil of aggregated wealth.

This much desired object can be accomplished only by the united efforts of those who obey the divine injunction, "In the sweat of thy face shalt thou eat bread."

Therefore, we have formed the order of Knights of Labor, for the purpose of organizing and directing the power of the industrial masses, not as a political party, for it is more—in it are crystallized sentiments and measures for the benefit of the whole people, but it should be borne in mind, when exercising the right of suffrage, that most of the objects herein set forth can only be obtained through legislation, and that it is the duty of all to assist in nominating and supporting with their votes, only such candidates as will pledge their support to those measures, regardless of party. But no one shall, however, be compelled to vote with the majority; and calling upon all who believe in securing " the greatest good to the greatest number," to join and assist us, we declare to the world what our aims are :

I. To make industrial and moral worth, not wealth, the true standard of individual and national greatness.

II. To secure to the workers the full enjoyment of the wealth they create, sufficient leisure in which to develop their intellectual, moral and social faculties : all of the benefits, recreation and pleasures of association ; in a word, to enable them to share in the gains and honors of advancing civilization.

In order to secure these results, we demand at the hands of the State :

III. The establishment of Bureaus of Labor Statistics, that we may arrive at a correct knowledge of the educational, moral and financial condition of the laboring masses.

IV. That the public lands, the heritage of the people, be reserved for actual settlers ; not another acre for railroads or speculators ; and that all lands now held for speculative purposes be taxed to their full value.

V. The abrogation of· all laws that do not bear equally upon capital and labor, and the removal of unjust techicalities, delays and discriminations in the administration of justice.

VI. The adoption of measures providing for the health and safety of those engaged in mining, manufacturing and building industries, and for indemnification to those engaged therein for injuries received through lack of necessary safeguards.

VII. The recognition, by incorporation, of trades' unions, orders and such other associations as may be organized by the working masses to improve their condition and protect their rights.

VIII. The enactment of laws to compel corporations to pay their employes weekly, in lawful money, for the labor of the preceding week, and giving mechanics and laborers a first lien upon the product of their labor to the extent of their full wages.

IX. The abolition of the contract system on National, State and Municipal works.

X. The enactment of laws providing for arbitration between employers and employed, and to enforce the decision of the arbitrators.

XI. The prohibition by law of the employment of children under 15 years of age in workshops, mines and factories.

XII. To prohibit the hiring out of convict labor.

XIII. That a graduated income tax be levied.

And we demand at the hands of Congress:

XIV. The establishment of a National monetary system, in which a circulating medium in necessary quantity shall issue direct to the people, without the intervention of banks; that all the National issue shall be full legal tender in payment of all debts, public and private; and that the government shall not guarantee or recognize any private banks, or create any banking corporations.

XV. That interest-bearing bonds, bills of credit or notes shall never be issued by the government, but that, when need arises, the emergency shall be met by issue of legal tender, non-interest-bearing money.

XVI. That the importation of foreign labor under contract be prohibited.

XVII. That, in connection with the post-office, the government shall organize financial exchanges, safe deposits and facilities for deposit of the savings of the people in small sums.

XVIII. That the government shall obtain possession, by purchase, under the right of eminent domain, of all telegraphs, telephones and railroads, and that hereafter no charter or license be issued to any corporation for construction or operation of any means of transporting intelligence, passengers or freight.

And while making the foregoing demands upon the State and National Government, we will endeavor to associate our own labors:

XIX. To establish co-operative institutions, such as will tend to supersede the wage system, by the introduction of a co-operative industrial system.

XX. To secure for both sexes equal pay for equal work.

XXI. To shorten the hours of labor by a general refusal to work for more than eight hours.

XXII. To persuade employers to agree to arbitrate all differences which may arise between them and their employees, in order that the bonds of sympathy between them may be strengthened, and that strikes may be rendered unnecessary.

THE DEMANDS OF LIBERALISM

as presented by the National Liberal League, Col. Robert G. Ingersoll president:

GENERAL OBJECT.

We have for our object the total separation of Church and State, so that equal rights in religion, in politics, and freedom and brotherhood in all human affairs may be established, protected and perpetuated.

As a means to accomplish this general object, we endorse the following nine demands of Liberalism:

1. That churches and other ecclesiastical property be no longer exempt from taxation.

2. That the employment of chaplains in congress, in state legislatures, in the army and navy, in prisons and asylums, and all other institutions supported by public money, shall be discontinued.

3. That all public appropriations for educational or charitable institutions of a sectarian character shall cease.

4. That all religious services sustained by national, state or municipal governments be abolished; especially the use of the bible in the public schools, whether ostensibly as a text-book or avowedly as a book of religious worship, shall be abolished.

5. That the appointment, by the president, or by the governors of the various states, of religious festivals, fasts, or days of prayer, being unconstitutional, shall wholly cease.

6. That the judicial oath be abolished, and that simple affirmation, under the penalties of perjury, be established in its stead.

7. That all laws directly or indirectly enforcing the observance of Sunday as the Sabbath shall be repealed :

8. That all laws looking to the enforcements of "Christian" morality be abrogated, and that all laws shall be conformed to the requirements of natural morality, equal rights, and impartial liberty.

9. That in the practical administration of the Constitution, either of the nation or the several states, no privilege shall be conceded to Christianity, or any other special religion — our entire political system to be founded and administered on a purely secular basis, and whatever changes shall prove necessary to this end, be consistently, unflinchingly, and promptly made.

CHAPTER V.

THE SPIRITUAL SCIENCES.

Modern Spiritualism is a science that establishes the facts that the spirits of mankind live after the death of the body, and communicate with the people of earth. This science rests on well established manifestations and communications, that have been heard and witnessed hundreds of times, by the most learned and devoted scientists and scholars, and thousands upon thousands of times by well informed people, who were not scientists, but good common sense people, and close observers of the works of nature and spirit. I will mention a few of these manifestations :

1st. Raps that show an intelligent spirit—often naming the spirit.

2nd. Writing, by spirits taking possession of the medium's mind, or only his hand, and writing good, intelligent messages ; and many messages are written by spirit power on slates, or paper, without the help of the medium in a physical way.

3d. The mediums lay their hands on the sick, by spirit directions, and they recover.

4th. Spirits speak through mediums and give the people spirit knowledge, and the most convincing tests of the spirit's presence and power.

5th. Spirits photograph themselves on the sensitive plate of the photographer.

6th. Spirits lift heavy bodies, and float mediums in the air.

7th. Spirits prepare mediums to handle burning coals of fire, and to put their hands and faces in the hottest flames, without injury to them.

8th. Spirits materialize so as to be recognized by their acquaintances, and they walk and talk with them.

9th. Spirits make mediums clairvoyant and clairaudient.

10th. Spirits are enabled by some mediums to bring flowers, plants, fruits and many other articles from a distance, into rooms where these mediums are.

11th. Spirits tie knots in an endless rope; take off from mediums their coats, when they are securely tied on and their hands tied together, and put them on again.

12th. Spirits make articles disappear from closed rooms, and reappear in another part of the room, or it may be they could not be found again.

13th. Spirits find lost articles and restore them to their owners.

14th. Spirits give information to individuals of the utmost importance to them in their business and personal matters, and they will give it to nations and people generally, when the seek to be just and true to all the people.

Many more kinds of communications might be mentioned, but persons wanting them, are referred to Epes Sargent's "Scientific Basis of Spiritualism," and other works by Prof. Hare, Judge Edmunds, Prof. Crooks, Wallace and Zoellner, for accurate scientific accounts of these various manifestations.

The teachings of these spirits are, that they know no more about a personal God than the people of the earth. The spirits are subject to the same law power of nature that the people are, who are in their earthly bodies, and they have no more control over these laws than people have in their bodies of flesh, but are subject to them and do all their works by the power these laws give them. Many of these spirits are as ignorant and superstitious as the most ignorant of the earth, and these are the spirits that Pagans, Jews and Christians have declared Gods, because they could do some marvelous works, or these works were done in their presence. Then they made Gods out of men and beasts, that they pretended these Gods had endowed with godly powers to raise the dead and do other miracles, by overpowering nature's laws. But as many persons are raised to life, who were apparently dead, when no persons were present, the conclusion is, that there never was a person that was really dead, that is, his spirit completely separated from the body, that ever was resuscitated, so as to inhabit his old body and live in it on earth. Spiritualists have continued to get spirit communications and rejected all gods but the law God of nature and spirit, and many seem to reject even that power as a God and make chance a God, instead of law; or, they reject the name of God, and yet have a supreme power. They are in a muddled state of confused ideas, and may be called spiritual atheists. They are without a basis to put a moral principle on, and yet are always talking of morals. They are without a basis to establish justice on, yet are always talking of justice. They are without a basis to establish humane principles, yet are always saying they want a humane religion and government. They are without a basis to establish truth upon, yet are always contending for the truth. I may be asked why I make these statements? Because there must be a power, that is constant, reliable and unchangeable, or there is no truth, no justice, no moral principles, no humanity, that is permanent. To-day it is right—to-morrow it is wrong. If you have a Pagan or Christian God that is changed by prayer, or an atheist one that is chance, you have no virtue to reward or vice to punish, with any certainty, because prayer, or the blood of Christ, or chance, may have changed it, and Christian Spiritualists and the atheist Spiritualists are in a muddle between the two. The spirits teach that there is a power permanent, relia-ble and unchangeable, that enables them to do their

48

work and governs them while doing it, as well as at all other times. This power they call God, and I find that as good a name as I have ever heard.

Most Spiritualists are contented with the fact that spirits communicate, and go to them for counsel. Such Spiritualists wonder why it is that there is such a division among them. The reason is plain : the spirits give different advice, and the brain of the world must take all this mixed advice and make harmony out of it, which never is done. It is the business of this age to see that it is done, and that the Spiritualists have a fair chance to adopt the true God, and make a just religion, organization and government.

This class of Spiritualists, keep it alive, among the most intelligent people in the country. It is so rooted in facts and in experience that it is constantly gaining and

The spirit's ceaseless tread, is lighter than noiseless air,
Their voices softer than finest harp, played by zephyrs fair,
Yet their voices and their tread, resound from pole to pole,
Like music in the spheres, is heard by every living soul.

Spiritualism is so strong in truth, and so majestic in the public feeling among the people, so pure in its teachings of justice and virtue, so undisguised in its principles and so fair in its statements, that it must always command the attention of the high, the low, the learned and unlearned. It joins the sciences and makes a religion, it joins the humane and makes a just and merciful government, it joins with the moral and establishes the science of morals, it joins with the best socialists to establish a just social science, it asks no privileges, immunities, pay or exemption from taxes by the government, only such as other religions have, and to have as much right to promulgate their doctrines among the people. If people are subject to fine and imprisonment for speaking against Christ and the Holy Ghost the same punishment should be meted out to those who speak against the truth, especially spiritual truth.

We say to the Christians, come out and expose the body of your religious principles and Word-God to the searching investigation that the spiritual doctrines are exposed to ; let us have no hiding behind gorgeous tapestry, flowery drapery, and flimsy pageantry, or college arts and university deceptions and theological frauds and pulpit persuasion and rhodmontade. Bring out your Christ God and see how he differs from our spirit mediums, bring out your Jewish God and let us see if he differs from our good and bad spirits, bring out your Devil and let us see if he differs from our spirits and spirit mediums that are called evil, bring forth your bible and let us compare its communications with the spirit communications of the present day, and learn the exact difference, and determine which is most true, most humane, most just, most sensible and which would be most likely to increase the intelligence and comfort of the people.

Let us compare the pulpit teachings of the Christian priests, with the platform teachings of spirit mediums and speakers, and learn which gives the most real instruction to their hearers ; then take up the works of standard authors of the Christians and compare their teachings with those of the Spiritualists, and when we have gone through comparing these religious systems and statements, we will compare them with justice, truth and righteousness in moral, social and religious ethics, and last and most important, what kind of a government do the religious principles call for ? Shall the laws be like the kingdom of heaven or like the republic of heaven? Shall the people have equal rights or the many be subject to the few ? These are very important religious questions.

There is no part of the religion, of which Spiritualism is the basis, that is so difficult to manage, as to prevent the adoption of saviours, Christs and Gods like all the old religions, and leave spirits and Spiritualism out in the cold. Soon after the spirit rappings became known, there were many Christs or Semi-Christs that presented themselves for leaders, and small bands of believers followed them. The modern Christs were modeled after the ancient. Those were the saved and righteous who followed them, and the persons who would not, were devils and damned. They imitated the Christ of the Christians most, and when these christs got very wroth, they called those that would not follow them Devils and the children of their father the Devil. See Emma Hardinge in her history of Modern American Spiritualism, Chapter 21.

The greatest number appeared in our conventions, but the great body of Spiritualists paid no more attention to them than they did to other mediums, because the spirits told them that the ancient Gods and Christs of religionists were abominations and frauds, got up by men to deceive the people, and their modern imitators were no better, and the prophecy is that modern Spiritualists will never switch off from Spiritualism, to a God or Christ, as all the old religionists did in making their religion, but will always ask for spirit information, of spirits and not conclude that one spirit knows it all. It is not consistent with the intelligence of the people of this age, but it is to make a common sense religion based upon scientific principles, and there is no probability that they will accept any other.

Now the question is, what are the teachings of the spiritual sciences. A spiritual science is founded on a spiritual law or laws, the same as a material science is, on a natural law or laws.

These sciences agree in the fact that they are founded on immutable laws, and both naturally teach the same religion and there never would have been any disagreement among people, if false gods had not been set up by priests, to enable them to rule the people instead of the true God and his agents, the spirits of heaven, and the most intelligent people of earth. Here I put in what has been declared the

RELIGIOUS TEACHINGS OF SPIRITUALISM.

Resolved,
That spirits teach.

That man has a spiritual nature as well as a corporeal, which spirit has an organized form composed of organs corresponding to those of the corporeal body.

That the spirit lives after the death of the physical body—in a spirit world as substantial to it, as this world is to our physical bodies.

That the mental constitution or moral character of persons is not altered by physical death.

That happiness or suffering in the spiritual state, as in this, depends on personal conformity to universal spiritual and physical laws.

That the experiences and attainments in this life, lay the foundation on which the next commences.

That since growth is the law of human beings in this life and in the spirit life, we infer an endless progression in the spirit life.

That the spiritual world is not far off, but near, around or inter-blended with our present state of existence. Hence we are constantly under the cognizance of spiritual beings.

That as individuals are constantly passing from the earthly to the spiritual state in all stages of mental and moral growth, the spirit world contains all grades of character, from the lowest to the highest.

That each of these shades of character gravitates to his own place of happiness or misery by the law of natural affinity. So that the seven spiritual spheres or many mansions, rather tend to confuse than to give a correct idea of spiritual life.

That communications from the spiritual world are not necessarily infallible truth. But on the contrary, partake of the imperfections of the minds from which they emanate and the mediums through which they come, and are liable to misapprehension by the persons who receive them.

Hence that no inspired communication in this or any age, is authority any further than it expresses truth to the person who receives it.

That inspiration, or the influx of ideas from spirits, is not a miracle of a past, but perpetual fact of all ages.

That all known angelic and demoniac beings, which have manifested themselves in the past, were disembodied human spirits.

That all authentic miracles (so called) in the past, such as raising the apparently dead, healing the sick by laying on of hands, and the movement of heavy bodies without visible power, have been produced by spirits in harmony with universal law, and can be repeated at any time under suitable conditions.

That the causes of all phenomena and the sources of all life, intelligence and love, are to be sought in the spiritual realm, not in the material.

That the chain of causation leads to an infinite spirit that pervades all matter, and by natural selection, under the laws of attraction and repulsion, makes all forms on earth and in heaven; and is the same principle in the divine mind as is love and wisdom among the wisest and best of mankind; and these dual laws are the fathers and mothers of mankind, and make them brethren.

That man as the offspring of this infinite parent is the most complete embodiment of this "Father's fullness" which we can contemplate, and is an incorruptible portion of the divine essence, which is ever prompting to the right, and which in time will free itself from all imperfections incident to its earthly condition.

That all evil is disharmony, more or less, with this divine principle, and was created to excite or induce people to get knowledge and turn evil into good. Ignorance is the greatest evil that ever afflicted mankind; and knowledge is the greatest good that ever came to them; and by it they can attain the greatest amount of happiness that can be enjoyed in time or eternity.

Resolved, That the hearty and intelligent conviction of these truths, with a realization of spiritual communication, tends:

To enkindle lofty desires and spiritual aspirations.

To deliver from painful fears of death and imaginary evil.

To give a rational conception of spirit life.

To stimulate to the worthiest employment of the present life.

To energize the soul to all that is good; and restrain it from all that is evil.

To guard against the degrading influence of impure spirits.

To promote our highest endeavors to purity of heart and life.

To stimulate the mind to the largest and freest investigations on all subjects.

To deliver from all bondage of authority, except to truth.

To make every man, more of an individual and more of a man.

And to make each one modest, courteous and deferential.

To promote charity and toleration for all differences of belief.

To cultivate and wisely direct the affectional nature.

To quicken the religious nature, making truth only acceptable.

To quicken all philanthropic impulses, stimulating to enlightened and unselfish labors, for the good of mankind, under the encouraging assurance that the exalted spirits of our race, instead of retiring to idle away an eternity of inglorious ease, are inspiring us to the work, and aiding it forward to a certain and glorious issue.

The above is an amended abstract of the platform of resolutions, adopted at the Spiritualistic convention held at Rochester, N. Y., August, 1868. It is a clear statement of the information spirits have given of themselves and their work in their heavenly home, and of the elevating and comforting influence they have on intelligent Spiritualists who commune with them. And the question naturally arises : What are those lofty desires, and high and noble principles ? They are answered in a general way in the resolutions. "It is to promote charity and toleration for all differences of belief," and "quicken them to the unselfish labors for the good of mankind." But it will be stated that other religions have made just such beautiful wordy promises, but wholly failed in establishing the special principles by which these glorious promises could be fulfilled. This being a historical fact, every intelligent person will naturally ask, what are the special moral principles that guide Spiritualists in their philanthropic work ? The following principles have been presented to many piritualists, and approved as containing the best special practical principles that have as yet been formulated to benefit mankind.

1st. You must get knowledge—of the God power and its laws. Of heaven and its spirit inhabitants. Of man and his necessities. Of wisdom and its ways.

2nd. You must give others the rights you claim for yourself. Or equal rights; to get knowledge and do just works in the pursuit of happiness. Man cannot form a just government until this principle is adopted.

3d. You must not damn or condemn a person for their belief or want of belief in any gospel, or any religion. Civilization is based on the principle that people are not condemned for wrong belief, but only for wrong acts.

4th. You must give persons the right at all times to express their opinions upon any subject, when it is done in order; and to put their opinions into practice when it does not interfere with the rights of others. The people who allow the greatest freedom of orderly speech and just works, are the most civilized. The ignorant and superstitious are easily led by heartless politicians, guided by bigoted priests, and lawless military chieftains, to stop persons from speaking the truth, or doing right.

5th. You must join with the spirits, to heal the wounded, cure the sick, give the greatest consolation to the sorrowing and afflicted, and bring your gifts to be expended in the best way to feed and clothe the poor and give them the comforts of life, and the greatest amount of knowledge that they are capable of receiving.

The test by which all religions must be judged, is the justice and truth of its principles, and the good deeds of its professors. The religion that presents the best precepts and practices is the nearest to God or the cause of all good, and the religion that presents the worst, is the nearest to the devil or the cause of all evil.

The spirits, with the mediums, protected by Spiritualists, have done more to cure the sick and comfort the people in all their woes of body and mind than the ministers of any other religion. Thus they have done their part in establishing the best religion that was ever given to mankind ; and now, if Spiritualists will do their duty as well, the spirits will pour out greater blessings on them than were ever bestowed upon any other people of the earth.

1st. Spiritualists must bring their gifts together to make a society, home, church, and educational institution all in one ; where the poor can be self-supporting without oppressive labor, and besides be afforded every opportunity to get a good education.

2nd. The Spiritualists donating the funds, should form a society, elect officers, especially trustees, to take charge of the funds and invest them in a society home, as directed by a unanimous vote of the members.

The object to be attained, is to establish a society home that is a heaven of harmony and love on earth. It is just as impossible to do this without individuals giving up a fair proportion of their property, as it is for them to go and dwell with the purest spirits of heaven without giving up their bodies and all their earthly possessions. And again, it is just as impossible to establish a society home that will make the members self-supporting and happy, without establishing the hours of labor, as it is for a company to be successful financially in any industrial business without a system, and regular hours when work must be done. In the final selection of persons to become resident members of the home, those must be chosen who are the most faithful in doing their duty, and are glad they are there to do it.

1st. The law of the home, is that resident members who are able, are expected to work eight hours per day for five days in a week ; it may be more in summer and less in winter. And two days each week are to be devoted to mental labor and recreation, for the same number of hours.

2nd. The hours of physical labor may be made less when there is over-production ; more than is required for a safety fund. And more hours may be required when absolutely needed. The object is for the poor laborers to partake of all the blessings of inventions and labor-saving machinery.

3d. As a general rule, members are expected to do their work between the hours of eight A. M. and five P. M. But work must be done before and after these hours, and such work will be assigned to those members who prefer to do it.

4th. Good and necessary work is the most sacred religious duty and worship that any person can perform, and visitors and idlers should be carefully instructed not to interrupt this necessary worship.

5th. That every resident member shall submit to a candid, friendly criticism, when other members or themselves request it, at meetings held for the purpose, and there shall be no reply to such criticisms at the meeting. The object is for each member to learn patience and know themselves as others know them, and be as just as the purest spirits of heaven.

6th. Marriages shall be civil contracts, the same as they are in heaven. Ownership of husband or wife shall be repudiated.

It will be seen that Christians end their organization where Spiritualists begin theirs. They organize to talk ; we talk and consider how to make the best organization. They adopt the principle that the body is cursed, and the spirit can only be blessed by faith. We, that the body is a blessed casket that holds a spirit that lives eternally, and both are worthy of our kindest consideration and care.

We worship knowledge; to learn to be just and fair.
And reject all the gods that ever were known.
We pray to the spirits, who answer our prayer.
While the gods are as dumb as their idols of stone.

We worship knowledge by working to get it. We worship the brotherhood of mankind, by working to make it a fact in practice. We do not call ourselves the children of God, and others "the children of the Devil." But we ask all people to join us and say, as the old translations are used on the pulpit :

Christians give us a decent book,
Let truth shine out wherever we look,
Not obscene, barbarous or vile,
Nor deceiving, like a villain's smile.

Shakespeare has been cleansed of its obscenities by women-readers, and those attending the theatres. Burns is prepared in the same way for the modern parlor, and ancient history is cleared of its falsehoods and obscenities, and fitted for our common schools. But the bible remains as obscene and false as it was made by the licentious and lying priests who lived between the second and sixth centuries.

Constantine and his adherents made Christ one of the gods of the Roman empire. The people and the emperor were cunning, deceitful, ignorant and brutal, and they chose their gods for like qualities, and the noble sentiment, "Let justice be done, though the heavens fall," was heard no more. Let us compare their God-Christ, elder brother, and ancient medium—as he is called—with a modern medium. A. J. Davis, at about seventeen years of age, commenced his spiritual work, and was taken by his spirit to the best of spirits; took council with them, was tempted by them, and was finally considered worthy to receive the magic staff that contained a remedy for every disease that afflicted humanity, and guided by its injunction " to always keep an even mind," he became a self-supporting gentleman, scholar and medium, boy as he was, that has no equal in history, or even fiction. He is the elder brother of all men in precepts and examples of wisdom and knowledge.

Jesus Christ was about thirty years old, a matured man, when he commenced his ministry, and his spirit took him to the Devil, to be tempted and get instruction, and he, like his tempter, became a boor in manners; and a poor weeping mendicant by precept and practice; and, after having sought this lowest, vilest company, and being in it forty days, he leaves it with an order worthy of any person who had gone to the Devil : "Get thee behind me Satan," and the dark spirit went behind him, and did his wonderful deeds; and the clairvoyants saw him, and told Jesus; and he denied it, in the coarse language the Devil had taught him : " That they were the children of their father, the Devil;" and he said to Peter, his most trusted and intelligent disciple, " get thee behind me Satan." Such a medium at this time would be considered obsessed by every intelligent Spiritualist, and medical experts would pronounce him insane; and, if he proceeded to arm his followers, as Jesus did, would have him put in an insane asylum. Yet Christians call him their God and Saviour, because the Romans made him one of the gods of their empire. Spiritualists, here are two mediums. One went to the Devil to be educated; the other to the purest angels. One teaches a theology about an unknown God; the other the philosophy of life and of living. One teaches you to obey the bible as the inspired word of God; the other to obey the laws of nature as the laws of God. One teaches you to pray to God, and preach and beg for a living; the other to pray to the spirits, get knowledge, and work for a living. Which will you choose for your elder brother, bosom companion and exemplar? Let us meet together in conferences and conventions this year, and declare the gospel of Spiritualism, its religious, moral and social teachings, and especially the form of worship which is most essential to saving body and spirit from pain and misery in this world and the summer land.

Psychology is the power one person or animal has over another, by means of their magnetic or electric force, with or without physical contact. Persons may be psychologized by intently looking at metals or other objects, or they may do it on themselves, by putting themselves in a negative condition, and making some passes over themselves, and may be without any movements, but merely by abstracting from the mind all thoughts, except wishing for the control. It may be a spirit which sometimes psychologizes the person. This is one of the most important ruling powers in animal life. It has always been felt, but its real power and importance has not been known until this age of science. Under a low grade of intelligence, it is the most powerful force to enable persons to establish despotisms. It is a blind force, that can be governed for good only by an intelligent, educated people. It is the beastly power men use, who teach that reason is dangerous.

They wish to keep people as ignorant and unreasoning as beasts; then they can rule people by the unreasoning forces of muscular strength and magnetic power.

PSYCHOMET^RY.

This is one of the most singular manifestations of spirit power ever brought to the notice of mankind. It shows that every particle of matter has life —has a soul that can hear, see and feel, and can store away in memory for thousands of years, and the psychometrist is told that history when he takes the pebble. It is found that dead matter, so called, is full of thoughts, full of life, full of every faculty of man, except his reason and executive power, and it may be that these are in every particle of matter, but so small in force as to be imperceptible by man. The proof that it has these faculties, is that man and beasts have them, derived from the spirit of matter. Another proof, is the orderly manner in which the sun, moon and planets are made and kept in their places. There seems to be the same orderly will-power, and reasoning power, that the best of human beings possess, to adopt this law of order and exact time for the movements of these great bodies in space. We find that in human affairs, ignorance makes great disorder among the people, even if presided over by the most intelligent people. So the intelligence of a God might not be able to keep in order the worlds in space, unless they possessed the highest intelligence. When we find that apparently dead matter has all the five senses of man, we do not have to stretch our imagination much, to conclude that the planets and heavenly bodies have more wisdom than was ever given to man, and more than man has the capacity to acquire.

This statement is made because large bodies seem to possess more power mentally and in every other way than small ones, and the inference is, that it takes all matter and spirit to have all knowledge and all the power and wisdom required to make a harmonious whole out of all nature and spirit and their products.

This soul reading is of the greatest value in the practice of medicine and in society. It prepares people to know at sight and touch, the character of persons; their diseases and the remedies, morally, socially and physically, that are required for them. In connection with Spiritualism, it is the great power to clear the world of cheats and frauds.

CHAPTER VI.

MENTAL SCIENCES AND INVENTIONS.

Mathematics is a purely mental science, and stands alone as an exact science ; by it man measures all things in heaven and earth. It is wholly made by mental calculations, and has no assistance, no support ; only man's mental action. There is a law of nature that man cannot control, but he can esti- mate the power and force of that law. There is not a known science that shows so distinctly the power and place of man, and the exact movements and unvarying force of nature's laws, as mathematics. If gravitation varied in power, Fairbank's scales could never have been made. If the movements of the heavenly bodies and the earth were not on exact time, clocks could not be relied upon and the science of astronomy could not have been made. But math- ematical calculations demonstrated that these forces were always the same, and the movements on exact time.

Now, is there in nature, the basis for a code of moral and just laws, that are as exact as those that make the laws of mathematics possible ? And can man find that basis as clearly as that science ? Are the rights of persons to life, liberty, property and the pursuit of happiness as clearly stated, and as well understood, as the rules of mathematics ? No. Why not ? The same God made the basis for both of these principles, and why has not man made as much progress in one as the other ? Simply because man has not been allowed the same liberty to investigate and make his experiments and observations to deter- mine what is moral and just, as he has to make math- ematical calculations. If you go back five hundred years among Christians, you will find they knew as much of one as the other. Since that time, the mathematicians have been allowed to study their science. But the moral scientists have not been allowed to live in peace only in the last few years, and never to make their experiments as they must do, to perfect their science. The demand now is, that they shall have the right, but it may be a long time before they will get it. It must be remembered that both these are mental sciences, and show the exact places where God's laws end, and man's laws begin and end.

LANGUAGES.

A person would hardly think that all the known languages of the people of earth have but about 50 sounds, and all those sounds can be distinctly uttered and represented in an alphabet, and yet such is the fact; showing that there is a law of sound that people can not violate in making their words to represent things. This shows that there is a basic law of language that people can not get by. This does not show that a word is God. But it does prove that man is governed by a God power in making words; yet, the words of all languages are made by man. The law-God of nature made the basis for these languages; there his work ended, and man made all the rest. It has taken people thousands of years to make these discoveries, with no legal preventatives. Now, give thinking people a chance to search in nature the basic principles for making moral and just law, and see if they will not make the discoveries, and adopt the principles and rules that will give them intelligence and harmony. This basic law "is the divinity that shapes our ends," and all people want, is a chance to find out how he shapes them and they will find it, morally and socially, as well as they have in languages, when they get their right by law and public opinion.

INVENTIONS.

Where do inventors look for the law to discover how to make useful inventions? The great distinguishing difference between this age and past ages, are the labor-saving inventions. Christianity remains the same. They still read, "servants obey your masters;" "wives be obedient to your husbands." They still wish to enslave men and women; there is no change in their talk and habits, when they can find people ignorant enough to listen to them. Then, where do these improvements come from? From infidels, who study nature's laws and wisely use the information they get. Their bible is the earth and nature's laws, not the book of words that priests tell them contains all knowledge and wisdom. The inventors of all ages have gone to the book of nature to get their knowledge and wisdom. We see the Mohammedans studying it in the Christian dark ages, when they invented algebra and made alphabets and numerals, which are used to-day. We see the Greeks studying it in their enlightened ages, when they made their great architectural structures, and their unequaled works of sculpture and painting. We see it among the Romans in the highest state of their civilization, just as we see it now in the decadence of their religions. Wherever we see a progressive people, there is to be seen religion on a back seat. This must always occur as long as the people have a religion that condemns nature as a devil, and classes the earth, the flesh and the devil as one and all evil, because all progress is made by studying the earth, the flesh, and the good and evil of life in nature. We are now in the heyday of progress and prosperity, inventions and discoveries are covering the land with blessings; the ancient divine books are being laid aside for the book of nature, and its revelations are wonderful to all people, and notwithstanding the bad religion and oppressive laws, that oppress the poor laborers of the land, yet the blessings are more wide-spread among all people than any religion ever permitted, or ever will be, unless it is made true to nature and nature's God, as manifested by the laws of nature. Until that time we shall have the torture and murder of such men as Servetus and Bruno, and the slanders and falsehoods of such men as Paine and Ingersoll. The very best of men and women will be slandered, tortured and murdered by Christians, because they are good, true and useful. It is not likely that they would hang a Mary Dyer in Boston now, as they did more than two hundred years ago, because she would speak her mind ; but they might in Delaware, and states south of it, as they have threatened Ingersoll. History gives but one character to all the sacrificial religionists, whether Pagan or Christian ; in one word, it is brutality. History gives but one character to scientists and inventors—they are reasoning humanitarians.

People must choose to have the inventor and knowledge and free thought, or the priest and ignorance and despotism over the thinking people. The invention of the art of printing is of more value to mankind than all the priests of all the religions of the world. The inventor enslaves the elements of nature, and makes them do the work imposed upon man when ignorant. The priests enslave the people and keep them ignorant, to prevent them from using their mental powers to make nature's laws do the work for mankind. Printing is the work of the Devil. Just think of it reader--this, the greatest blessing ever given to man, is a Devil, so pronounced to-day by priests to ignorant people. The invention of the telescope, by which we survey the heavens, is of more value to mankind than all the priests in the world, and the same may be said of the microscope. It is no great stretch of the imagination to conclude that in due time people will see the spirits with the natural eye and hear them with the natural ear. Such a wonder is foreshadowed by the discovery of the

ECHO FASTENER.

There is one curious discovery made by Edison, the inventor. It proves that matter will retain a sound. Psychometrists have discovered it, by taking pieces of rocks and other articles. This discovery is different. A person makes a speech in presence of his phonophone, and it is recorded in sound and can be repeated like an echo, at any time, by running the paper containing it through the instrument. This is made plain to common ears. In this way, the speeches of to-day can be repeated in time to come, when the people wish to hear the voices of the departed, as near the original as an echo is to the voice that makes it. Since Spiritualism has become a factor in human affairs, it has been discovered that, although the laws of nature and spirit are unchangeable, what are called cursed by priests and their ignorant followers, are turned into blessings by the intelligent inventor and his spirit friends. They make the lightning work for us. They make dead matter, so-called, give us information. The voice of a speaker, in a low tone, is plainly heard many miles away. By the inventors, news is conveyed around the world in a few minutes. Any one of these inventions is of more value to mankind, in saving them hardships and pain, than all the priests that ever lived. Which will you have : Ignorance, misery, and the priests, or intelligence and comfort, with the inventor ?

REASON.

Reason is the highest gift that the God of nature ever gave to man. It is the best gift man can think of. It is by this gift alone that there ever can be peace on earth among the people. This is well known among all thinking people, yet it never has been the basis of any great religion. The priests have always substituted inspiration and belief or love in the heart, instead of reason and facts in the head. They always speak to the heart when they wish to cause a revival interest among the people, to induce them to join their church and pay the preacher. If these ministers and priests would spend half as much time in reasoning from facts, as they do in persuading people to be governed by their hearts, they would not be the worst people in the world, as they now are. The head is put on top, to be in the best position to take charge of the body, and be the best guide and controlling power in the human system. The heart is put under it to give us warnings ; they may be true or false alarms. The preachers are constantly dwelling on these alarms, and nine out of ten of them are false warnings, or false alarms. They have thrown away all the God-given head work, mind work, and reasoning work, to employ all their powers in prepar-

ing warnings and alarms, until they have made des-
pair to rankle in the heart of the victim ; then they
calm the same by hope, and the insane are left in
their hopeless condition, to wander in body and mind
under the influence of their hearts, until their heads
are given control--if they ever become sane. There
is no other class of people on earth that are constantly advising persons to beware of reason, and be
guided by warnings, only preachers and priests, and
there is no other class of people so wrong, so wicked.
They stand at the gateway of all knowledge, with
their flaming, two-edged sword, ready to slay every
person who tries to enter there. Oh, ye people ! look
at the great heaps of slain that lay before the gates
of all the temples of knowledge. What were they
murdered for ? Simply because they sought knowledge, that they might be guided by the headlights of
reason and wisdom, and establish the merciful laws
of justice and truth, with a religion of wisdom and
government of just equality. Their only crimes
were, that they were virtuous and just. Civilization
is made by reasoners, barbarism by priests. Which
will you have, teachers or preachers ?

CHAPTER VII.

MATERIAL SCIENCES, MEDICINE AND LAW.

ASTRONOMY.

Astronomy is the science of the skies; a science that proves all things, and holds fast to that which is good and true. The professors of this science look at the sun, moon and stars, to learn what they are; how they are held in their place, and what relation they have to the earth. Could a more innocent employment be thought of? Why did the lord of heaven and earth set those brilliants in the heavens, if it would be wicked to look at them and calculate their character, uses, distances, and their movements? Yet, because men did this, they were put down as the most wicked sinners on the face of the earth, and tortured and burnt to death by the Christian priests, who proclaimed themselves the most intelligent, best and most holy persons in the world. Here were scientists, that had done nothing but obey the best of commands, who were tortured and murdered for it by the persons who published the command.

What could be the object of men in proclaiming such a duty for people to do, and then murdering them for doing it? The only just inference to be drawn is, that these priests consulted together, to proclaim the best of doctrines, and if people literally and fully obeyed them, and they could not stop them by other means, they must murder them. There was no other way to save the Christian priesthood and the bible. They said in their hearts, "we know there are more falsehoods than truths in our bible, but it must be sustained as God's truth." Some of the priests of that time knew that the past priesthoods had been founded on falsehoods, and they could not see the value of priests to a people who knew the truth; a priesthood was only supported by the ignorant, the superstitious, and those whose intent it was to keep people ignorant and superstitious.

Intelligent people want teachers to give them instruction, not preachers to deal out ancient false ideas about God and the world and the heavens, and the spirits of heaven and earth ; and the most intelligent priests knew their bible conveyed false ideas on every subject, and some of them would suffer tortures rather than proclaim falsehoods as truth. This is the reason that the priests are the worst of learned people in the world, because no intelligent good persons that are not forced to get their living by proclaiming these doctrines, will do it. But the wicked make the most genial tools for priest-craft to use to deceive the people, and make them murder astronomers and other searchers after truth and justice, to guide all the people of the earth.

GEOLOGY.

Geology is a science that teaches people how the earth was formed and prepared for man. It proves that it took millions of years in preparing, and was so unexpected, that it struck the priesthood with a deadly thud. They had killed so many thousands of people to prove that God made it in six days, and now to have people open the book of the earth, made by another God, and that these murders proved them revengeful supporters of lies, and they had very little chance to kill people for proving these lies on them. This was too much for them. We may say this was the first time the Christian priesthood was defeated in killing their enemies, for all are their enemies who seek knowledge outside their bible and its priests. Then to have it done by their order; to prove all things, and they not have any chance to murder them for it, as they had the chemists and astronomers was unbearable.

The priests had been defeated in many skirmishes before, but never in a regular mental battle. This time they were driven from the field, because the people had become sufficiently intelligent to occupy all the ground of truth that the priests had proclaimed they stood upon. But when put to the test, it was proved they did not stand upon proved truth, as they had declared, but on their claim of self-righteousness, and the persons who disputed this were to be silenced by every cruelty the priests could inflict. This complete and overwhelming defeat of the Christian priesthood shows the exact value of Christianity.

It proclaims some grand truths, and then some infamous falsehoods, and then approves of the persons who adopt the falsehoods, and punishes the persons who adopt and practice its truths, to the full extent that the laws and public opinion will permit. Christian Protestantism is as bad as Christianity in essence, but it cannot act as bad, because scientific Protestantism is mixed with it, and prevents tortures and slanders from being so cruel.

CHEMISTRY.

This is a science that shows the attraction and repulsion of atom to atom. By it, people learn that there is an invariable law that rules, and persons who wish to get a knowledge of this science, must study its laws, and not rely upon special providences in conducting their experiments. Chemistry takes into consideration the movements of the ultimate invisible atoms of matter, and the power that moves them, and finds there is an intelligent principle attached to every particle of matter that directs it where to go and where to stay, and when to move and when to be stationery. It finds that every particle of this matter has the wisdom of a God, but they do not find a few particles of this matter, combined with spirit that are made into a personal God. They find a designing law, but not a designing God back of that law. They find that a certain kind of matter and spirit makes a mental brain power, that is superior to any on earth, except the power that made the brain, and that power they find in every atom of matter.

The crystalization of various substances shows the beauty and intelligence of dead matter, so called. Each substance has sufficient knowledge to always

assume the same shape! Common salt has one
shape, alum another, and so on; and if chemistry
proves anything of a God power, it is, that it exists
in all spirit and matter that is in all space, and never
talks, but works silently by laws. It seems there is a
life to the crystal that gives it shape and size, the
same to man, animals and vegetables.

BOTANY

teaches how exact nature's laws are, as in the growth
of the different kinds of vegetation, the different
classes and orders, are known readily, and yet none
are exactly alike of the same order. The laws that
govern their growth and decay are fixed so that by
close observation one species can be distinguished
from another. But to describe these species that are
different, yet so near alike, that a language of botany
is required, with exact terms,. to enable persons to
distinguish one species from another. The study of
botany is the best of any science to learn persons to
be exact and correct in their language, in describing
events, actions and things. It shows that English
words and language will not answer to make a scientific language, but the dead languages must be used.
Yet, its study is of great advantage to make people
use the best of terms in their descriptions, in the
English language.

ZOOLOGY, OR THE SCIENCE OF ANIMAL LIFE,

shows that animals are under the law of order and
progress; that the law of their production and
growth is fixed for each species. Wherever you find
animal life, whether in worm, insect, fish, bird or
other animal, all are found to exist by a law of
nature, and bound by the laws of nature to have
certain forms, and to live certain kinds of life, and
to have a certain amount of freedom, and no more
freedom than their physical force gives them, or their
spiritual and physical forces combined give them.

Wherever man looks in life or death, there is a law of nature and spirit that rules, and whoever thinks there is a miracle God, that can rule this law God, has no proof of his existence. Yet all priests of all religions base their creeds and sermons upon the assumed facts that a miracle God is at the helm of power and runs the world, and the universe of worlds and people. While the scientific religionists proves by all nature and spirit that there is no other power that ever did or ever can rule nature's laws while this natural power exists.

THE MEDICAL PROFESSION,

like Protestantism, is based partly on facts and partly on theoretical guesses. They are seeking to have special powers granted to them that they may have a legal monopoly of the pay given by the sick to the doctors. They know their practice is no more scientific than the priests' preaching. This makes them anxious, like the priests, to secure by law, favors which they have no claim for in justice.

There is a law of diseases; there is a law of the action of remedies on diseases, but the action in many cases is so illy understood, that much of the practice is guess work or quackery.

THE LEGAL PROFESSION

has grown up under Protestant rule, and is just like it—professedly true and just, while practically, it is false and absurd; cruel beyond the conception of plain, fair people, but a vast improvement on the times when the priests were the lawyers, doctors, priests and executioners. When Protestantism ends in the age of science, these professions will stand according to their uses in establishing truth and justice in society. Keeping them at the front as the guide of the people until the age of science is established, and not allowing them to assume as great despotism as the priests had in their day of power, is the great work of this Protestant age.

All material sciences are based upon an unchangeable law of nature. Without this basis, these sciences could not be made, and as they are the surest guide mankind have discovered, to show the true character of the deity that rules the earth, and the true relation of man to the laws that are this deity, or that do his works and display his power and unchangeable order.

CHAPTER VIII.

PEACE OFFERINGS.

Shall we smoke the pipe of peace like the Indian, or declare the principles of peace and abide by them, like a civilized people? Shall we submit our minds to reason, as a peace offering, or to inspiration? Are the offerings of beasts, birds, or man, or their blood, as good to make peace on earth among people, as to study to be just, and to establish the laws of justice? Is the belief in Christ a better peace offering than a belief in virtue and goodness? Is the belief in Gautama, Confucius, Mohammed, or in all the gods and goddesses, and all prophets and prophetesses of ancient and modern times, Jewish and Christian, taken singly or collectively, as good a peace offering as the rules of simple justice? What is the best peace offering? Tell us, oh ye pious, oh ye learned, oh ye wise, oh ye of the most profound knowledge! Do the nine demands of liberalism contain this precious jewel? Do the twenty-two articles of the Knights of Labor hold it? Is it contained in the articles proposed in this book? Can we pick it out of the communications of spirits, ancient or modern? Let us consult our spirit friends about it, and reason together, and search the heavens and earth to find it. It is possible it may be found in knowledge and wisdom. It is certainly safe to look for it there, and to set all people to getting knowledge and using it wisely. We know, the more ignorant a people, the more they are given to quarreling and war, and where all the people are the best informed there is the most peace.

But the full benefit of the peace that is contained in knowledge has not had a chance to show itself, because in all countries it has been overshadowed by a militant church and state. When a person is engaged in getting information, the mind is being trained to peaceful pursuits, yet all knowledge is not calculated for a peaceful offering. Only special parts of it are fitted to be most beneficial in that line; such as the laws of life; the laws of society; the laws of association; the laws of peace, truth and justice.

Some reformers are opposed to making laws to suppress individual vice, and promote individual virtues; that such laws are opposed to individual liberty, which is of vastly more importance to secure, than anything that man can do by law. Right here is a difference of opinion about where personal liberty ends and society security begins. The object of law is to protect the innocent against the oppression of the wicked, and to protect the weak from being oppressed by the strong. Right here is wanted the peace offering that will unite the two parties who are seeking for justice to the weak and the strong, and to the innocent and the guilty, or those who would be guilty if not prevented by a just public opinion made into law, to be a better guide of that public opinion in suppressing vice and wrong, and promoting virtue and justice among the people. This is the special advantage of law. It not only instructs people to know the right from the wrong, but it guides them how to justly suppress wrong, and to take care of the wrong doer.

Some people say it is a vice and a crime to drink intoxicating drinks; others say it is good, and gives health and happiness. Some persons say that chewing and smoking tobacco is one of the greatest vices; others say it gives them health and strength, and they know it is a great good. Some persons say that eating pork is a great vice; that it is concentrated scrofula and disease. Others say that it is the finest meat that can be set before them. Infidels say that reading the Christian's bible and attending their meetings is one of the greatest vices of the age, because their bible is a nest of falsehoods, and the preacher knows it, and yet he reads it as truth, and threatens them that hear him with the direst of woes if they do not believe it true, and promises them the greatest of happiness if they will believe these falsehoods are truth. The Christians proclaim their bible and their meetings the greatest peace offerings ever presented to mankind. The Christians say the statements of infidels, that are proved true, are the greatest curses that ever visited the earth. The infidels say these statements are the greatest blessings and the best peace offerings ever presented to mankind. Christians and infidels say that spirit communications are the greatest of humbugs and inculcate the most gross superstitions of the age. Spiritualists believe these communications are the greatest blessings now known as peace offerings to all people; that by them and through their influence, harmony will be established and war will be heard of no more among the people of the earth.

Amongst all these conflicting opinions and interests, who can give the truth that will disorganize the contestants that are combating each other and organize them by an agreement on a peaceful basis; to adopt trial laws, where they can not agree upon what are just ones, or do not know how to frame laws that will be just, and make trial organizations to learn, as well as we can, how we should associate to live the best lives and do the most good? Let it be distinctly understood that the legislatures of all the states and territories and the congress of the United States of America be petitioned to sanction these trial laws and associations, when they are based upon the equal rights of their men and women adult citizens, and upon the moral principles that naturally attach to such citizen rights.

Suppose these petitions are not granted, what then is to be done? Make the associations and live the most virtuous lives that can be under present laws, and if there is a Servetus or a Mary Dyer that oversteps the laws so much that they are ordered burnt or hung, to satisfy present laws and Christian modes of thought and action, there will be nothing new for Christians about it, and the hope is that it will be the last of their inhumanity to man. Let us walk steadily forward in the path of progress, until there is a religion established that allows the good to live and make their experiments, and make a state that agrees with it.

The greatest peace offering ever presented to the nations of the world, is the science of free speech, in the shape of parliamentary laws, presented by the great sturdy men of England, in a line of noble men that continued for ages and centuries. They held to the equal rights, to free speech in parliament. Now as England and Englishmen have presented the best in their age, it becomes America and Americans to present the best in this age. That is the science of free rights, in the shape of equal rights in making the laws, and equal rights by the laws, after they are made. The declaration of independence proclaims the foundation of these principles, and it is the duty of the sturdy noble men and women of America to offer this greatest peace offering the people have ever thought of and the world has ever seen, so people may know how to make peace on earth and good will among men.

The best religious peace offering to be made, that I can present to the reader, is, to see if there is any God power, that all agree is the best and most reliable, because it is the most powerful and controls all things, and one that there is no power in heaven or earth, that can influence, or make deviate an iota from its laws and movements. All religious differences now are based on the different gods they worship or their different ways of managing the world, the flesh and the devil. Can any one point any other power that is immutable but the power of nature, the laws of nature? If people will imitate this God in being peaceful, in order, on times, under just law, as astronomy proves the God of nature to be, and be harmonious under the laws of attraction and repulsion as chemistry proves the God of matter to be, and allow the regular order of progression to go on as geology proves the God of nature has done, there will be peace on earth, among the people, and rejoicing that they have found a God that always makes peace by his laws and works in all time and space where man has no power to act. He has given man power to make and worship false gods and bring on strife and war, and that is what they have done, instead of adopting the true God and just laws and studying the acts of peace.

As one of the greatest peace offerings that the best of people can present, is the plan of the scientists to worship truth instead of the God of truth. They are always seeking for truth in all the works of nature, they worship natures laws instead of the God of nature's laws, because they know something of these laws certainly, and nothing certain of any God who has any management of them ; they worship justice instead of the God of justice, and this makes them call for the laws of justice to establish a government on just principles, they worship the laws of right and righteousness, instead of the God of right, because their law God has given them power to learn right from wrong, and not the power to consult with him by word, and learn what is right or wrong ; this is learned by experience and reason ; they worship the law of mercy instead of the God of mercy.

The question may be properly asked why they worship these laws and principles and not the God that stands for them. The reason is : laws and principles never give orders for unjust punishments, while the God that people cause to stand for the laws, does order the most cruel and unjust punishments. Such as he who breaks the Sabbath day shall not live. For hundreds of years scientists have been making these peace offerings to Christians, and they at first murdered them for it, then they reviled them, now they acknowledge the truth and justice of their course but reject it as a peace offering, while the Spiritualists accept it as the most wise and lovely, just and truthful peace offering ever presented to mankind for their guide to peace and harmony.

CHAPTER IX.

CONCLUSIONS.

False are the men of high degree,
The baser sort are vanity,
Weighed in a balance, both appear,
Light as a puff of empty air,"

This was the beginning of one of the sacred songs of the sturdy heroes of the revolution, when they beat from our shores George III., men of high degree and the baser sort. All their sacred songs in that day were like fuges and bid defiance to enemies ; this should be the position of reformers of this age. If men have one particle of unjust power by law, you may expect they will abuse all the people, that the power gives them a chance to subject to abuse. This any one can see, if they will look at the history of the slave masters, ruling over the slaves, and the people of this country. The same kind of history is made by the republican party after ten or fifteen years of power. They made a financial crash that is a disgrace to the men in power, and would be a disgrace to any financiers ; gave the ballot to the ignorant negroes and refused it to their intelligent mothers and sisters at the same time, acknowledging their claim was just and they should not long be subject to the negroes. But the longer they were in power the more abusive they became of women and wages working people.

When we look over the demands and platforms of the reform parties, they all agree in asking for their just rights, nothing more and nothing less will be accepted. The men in power to-day, are as false to their professions, as were the tools of George III. in his day. · The same rigthts are demanded and none oppose their being granted but ignorant stupids and knaves, just the same now as it was in the revolutionary war. The object to be attained, is not to

have men with a high degree of power nor a baser
sort for them to rest their claims on.

Let it be distinctly understood that there never
has been a great general of an army, since the fabu-
lous Cincinnatus, that gave equal rights to his
soldiers and citizens after he had cleared their
country of its public enemies. He has always loaded
favors upon favorites and made the people work and
foot the bills. Our soldiers homes are an illustration
of this kind of care for faithful crippled men ; they are
under despotic military law and can not speak to an
officer of their grievances without danger of being
locked up for it, and treated like a criminal. In view
of the treatment of great generals, to their common
soldiers, who obeyed their orders and achieved for
them the greatest honors the world can give, what
other conclusion can be reached but that the generals
hate their faithful soldiers in peace, the same as
slave-holders hate their slaves when they are freed,
and the same as tyrannical husbands, fathers and
brothers, hate women when they have equal rights
with men. Despots, in all times, have one mark in
all the world : They hate bitterly, people who are
striving for their just rights.

What is the matter with the great and little
people ? with the knowing among the ignorant? Are
they totally depraved as said by Christian priests, or
only depraved by their ignorance or surroundings ?
The proof seems to be that ignorance is the cause—
knowledge the cure, as the more a people of a state or
nation become educated, the less the depravity of the
great and small, because the great middle class, whose
interest is to have justice done, cause it to be done
nearer than in other states. The greater the ignorance among the people, the better is the chance for
the wicked to show their depravity, and they do it.

As education increases depravity ceases, and
the probability is that it will not exist when the
people become well informed. The religion and
governments of to-day are founded on intense love
and intense hate, and rewards and punishments are
meted out accordingly. All reformers of every party
ask for rights. In this they all agree, and they should

have them. Then they would moderate their love and hate, so that there would not be the least sign of depravity to be found about them. The law that is bad, is worse than any bad act made under it, because it stands for all the bad acts caused by it.

There is no excuse for the persons who will not grant these rights, except they believe in the total depravity of man, angels and their God. If the successful general believed in a just God, why is not his first act, after his soldiers have conquered the enemy, to give his soldiers their just and equal rights and extend such rights to their mothers and daughters and all faithful citizen? Why do not great statesmen and priests extend these rights to all citizens, especially when they ask for them, petition for them? Simply because their God is so depraved that he has not made in nature or spirit a law that enables man to make laws that will be just and equal to all mankind. But these depraved, cursed soldiers, sailors, citizens and women can give to the generals, statesmen and priests, just rights, riches and honors and all the blessings of heaven and earth ; and now when the common people are asking these rulers, if they can not afford to give them a fair and equal share of these rights, they have nothing but shotguns, threats and abuse to give them. These abuses have induced the common people and common soldiers to unite to demand their rights. They believe in a God who is as friendly to the common people as to those of high degree. That there are fixed and immutable laws of nature and spirit, that, if adhered to, will guide persons to make laws that will give just and equal rights to all people who will adopt them in practice. To secure these rights I present the following principles and laws for the consideration of the people :

1st. There are fixed and immutable laws of nature that are unchanged by time or prayer, upon which man can base true and just moral laws to guide and govern mankind.

2nd. We have communications from our spirit friends, by natural and spirit laws, informing us that they have in spirit spheres the same kind of spirit laws to guide and govern them, that are true, just and moral to them.

3d. To enable all people to learn what these immutable laws are, and man's duty under them, and to enable them to know where God's laws end and man's laws begin, and what man's laws shall be, to be in harmony with these laws of deity, we adopt the following laws and principles to guide them in this work :

1st. We adopt the science of free speech ; as interpreted by parliamentary law, as the guide of all people who engage in discussing the questions that arise about what is just and true.

2nd. We adopt the principles of the declaration of independence and parliamentary laws, that all adult citizens, male and female, shall have equal rights to life, liberty, property and the pursuit of happiness.

When the people have adopted these two laws, as their constitutional guide in making laws to regulate families, associations, religions and governments and in all conditions of life, there will be a firm foundation for people to be just in all their transactions. The most important laws that occur to me that come under this head, are :

1st. That wages-working peaple shall have fair living wages for their work. This pay to be determined by what it costs to live comfortably.

2nd. Great incomes to single individuals must be taxed, so that they cannot oppress the poor. A graduated income tax is considered the best.

3d. Great landed estates must be taxed out of existence.

It should be remembered that it was the persons who paid the working people only the poorest of food and clothing and house accommodations, and when they complained paid them in bloody stripes on their bare backs, and those who had great incomes and great landed estates, that declared a rebellion against the best government the world has over known, and these classes are always planning and trying all sorts of deceptions and frauds to establish unjust laws and institutions to make people ignorant and their willing tools. This brings us to the most important subject that the people can take hold of now.

4th. Resolved that every state and territory of this Union shall tax the property of their states or territory to establish common schools, so that all children of schoolage shall have a fair chance to get a common school education. If they refuse or neglect to do it, they should be deprived of a representation in congress, and the states turned into territories; and the United States should see to it that the people are taxed and the children educated, because it is well established that the ignorant cannot maintain a republican government, and those rulers should know that congress has as much right to turn men and states out, as they have to go out, as they did years ago.

Scientists, thinkers, Spiritualists and reformers are these nine propositions and principles true and just? Will they make the best foundation that man can conceive at this time, to establish the true religion and just associations and governments upon? If they are not, let us have the true ones, and then proceed to make special laws that are required to guide people in their special duties in life. Or if more general laws are required, before we can safely proceed to make special laws and rules, let us have them. It is the duty of governments to make special laws to protect individuals and associations in their rights, and it is the duty of every individual and association to obey all the just laws that governments enact for their guide, but never to obey an unjust law, only under protest, where the law is flagrantly unjust. The just law should be proclaimed with sufficient force to draw public attention to it. It is often said that we have too many laws. This may be true of bad laws, but not of good ones. Experience has proved that it requires between 300 and 400 laws to secure free speech in legislative bodies, all good and needed; a less number would not secure free speech. To secure the same freedom of rights, in all the affairs of life, how many laws it will take is not known, but all the laws should be enacted that are required. Whenever they want a law to secure the rights of members in legislative bodies, they make it. The same rule must be adopted by the people to establish the rule of justice as the law of the land.

Associations must have their special laws to guide them in their formation, and in paying the working partners in them. When such associations are religious, special laws will be required to enable them to have their worship. When they adopt the scientific religion, all good work is good worship, and besides this, they will assemble in circles to get counsel from the spirits. It will require gifts to the amount of about $50,000 to lay the proper foundation for a community of from ten to twenty families, that is, an association of from 50 to 100 persons.

If the Christians wish to raise that amount to build them a house and buy the grounds, they get it in a few days in this city; but all the free religionists united, in this union, will not be able to get such an amount in a year, to form an association to make experiments for a scientific free religious association, unless some one person will give the whole amount. Such is the result of experience. The church militant, or fighting church, is popular now, but the religion of science, of truth, justice and peace, has very little financial influence at this time.

The capital of this government should be removed to some point near the banks of the upper Mississippi, in a healthy location, among the intelligent, educated people of that section, to give congress a fair field to make a just government. It is clearly shown that the only time when the southern states made a marked improvement in education, was when they were being whipped by the northern people and the negroes, and were under negro and carpetbag rule. We want the capital in a section of the country where the people have not been debased by despotic laws and rulers. There is no hope that Spiritualism or the religion of science can prevail, only in enlightened countries, and we should make our head centres amidst such a people in North America, and invite representatives from all sections of the continent to come and counsel with us and assist us in finding out all the principles of righteousness, and adopting them to be the guide of all people, and if Christians kill the people for telling the truth, as they have in the past, they only prove that now; as formerly, they kill the truest and best people in the world to save the worst.

The great object in presenting this little work to the public, is to get people to reasoning together upon the foundation principles that make just associations and governments and the true religion, and to adopt them as their guide. I wish them to know that liberty consists of order and obedience to just laws, and slavery consists of disorder and obedience to unjust laws, and when I see people assembling together, to hear all kinds of laws, principles and propositions for the purpose of selecting the best to be their guide in establishing justice and making peace among the people, I shall be satisfied that my efforts have not been lost to the world, and it will be an abundant reward for the publication of this work.

INDEX.

III

ERRATA.

On page 13, second line from the bottom, insert "to make" before the words "a true religion."

On page 33, fourth line from the top, read "espouse" instead of "expose."

www.ingramcontent.com/pod-product-compliance
Lightning Source LLC
Chambersburg PA
CBHW020303090426
42735CB00009B/1201